Roosevelt Field
THROUGH TIME

Roosevelt Field

Through Time

A Visual History of a Historic American Airport

RICHARD PANCHYK

America Through Time is an imprint of Fonthill Media LLC
www.through-time.com
office@through-time.com

Published by Arcadia Publishing by arrangement with Fonthill Media LLC
For all general information, please contact Arcadia Publishing:
Telephone: 843-853-2070
Fax: 843-853-0044
E-mail: sales@arcadiapublishing.com
For customer service and orders:
Toll-Free 1-888-313-2665

www.arcadiapublishing.com

First published 2021

ISBN 978-1-63499-352-4

Typeset in Mrs Eaves XL Serif Narrow
Printed and bound in England

Foreword

by Reeve Lindbergh

In May of 1977 I visited Eisenhower Park, near the site of the original Roosevelt Field, with my mother. She had been invited to a celebration of the fiftieth anniversary of my father's historic non-stop solo flight from New York to Paris in the little silver monoplane, *The Spirit of St. Louis*. He was twenty-five years old at the time.

Following his transatlantic adventure, my father traveled around the United States for several months in his newly famous aircraft, promoting the brand new field of aviation. In December of the same year, he flew to Mexico at the invitation of U.S. ambassador to that country, Dwight Morrow. He spent Christmas with the Morrow family, and met the Morrow children, including the Morrows' middle daughter, Anne. She married him in 1929. He taught her to fly, and she became his co-pilot, navigator, and radio operator when the young couple traveled the world together to survey air routes for the fledgling aviation industry. They were married for close to half a century until his death in 1974, and raised five children together. I was their second daughter and their youngest child.

At the time of the fiftieth anniversary celebrations of the flight, my father had been dead for only three years, and his loss was still fresh for the family. In speaking about him during the many scheduled events around the country, we wanted to celebrate his life and character as we knew him, long after the famous flight. We knew, above all, his great love for the natural world and his hope that human beings could learn to balance our extraordinary technological advancements with care for our home, the earth. As my mother said, "He saw the enormous changes man had made on the earth's surface and which, if continued, would destroy the planet." He watched the earth beneath his wings in every airplane he flew, throughout all the years of his life. It was the pilot's view that gave him the perspective and the passion for the preservation of the earth.

In a sense, everything started at Roosevelt Field, where my father and his *Spirit of St. Louis* took off for France on a rainy morning in May of 1927. On the fiftieth anniversary of that flight, a replica of the *Spirit* flown by Paul Poberezny of the Experimental Aircraft Association circled high over our heads, and Deputy Postmaster General William Bolger presented an anniversary stamp featuring the *Spirit of St. Louis* flying over a dark ocean, against a bright blue sky.

Today the airplane hangs in the Smithsonian National Air and Space Museum, in the company of the Wright brothers' airplane and other historic aircraft, including the Lockheed Sirius my parents flew together in their survey flights. I visit the museum from time to time, just to be in the company of the *Spirit* and its companions.

I have never seen Roosevelt Field as it was in my father's day, because the field itself was sold for commercial purposes in 1951. However, I have been fortunate enough to visit the Cradle of Aviation Museum, a magnificent institution in nearby Garden City, where the numerous galleries and exhibits feature more than 100 years of aviation history, some of it made at Roosevelt Field.

Roosevelt Field was used as a take-off point not only for my father but for other pioneering aviators, including Amelia Earhart and Wiley Post. Even earlier, it was a training field (Hazelhurst Field) for the Air Service, United States Army during World War I.

I am so grateful to Richard Panchyk for his thoughtful and meticulously researched new book, which brings back to us all the excitement of this country's early aviation adventures and adventurers, and gives us a real sense of the special place where my father's story and so many other aviation stories began.

Reeve Lindbergh, May 2021

Reeve Lindbergh is the youngest child of Charles Lindbergh, and the author of *Under A Wing* and *No More Words: A Journal Of My Mother, Anne Morrow Lindbergh*

Acknowledgments

Thanks to Alan Sutton and Kena Longabaugh at America Through Time for their continued support. Thanks to Matt for accompanying me on some Roosevelt Field adventures.

Photo credits

National Archives: p22 bottom, p23-25, p26 top, p27 bottom, p28-39, p40 top, p46, p47 bottom, p48, p49, p50 top, p55 top, p60 bottom, p64, p72 top, p74-76, p83 top, p87 bottom.

U.S. Geologic Survey: p90, p93, p94, p98 bottom, p99 top, p101 bottom.

Library of Congress: p14, p15, p16 bottom, p17, p18, p19 bottom, p20-21, p26 bottom, p27 top, p50 bottom, p51, p52, p53, p55 bottom, p57 bottom, p58 top, p59 bottom, p63 bottom, p72 bottom.

All other images courtesy of the author.

Introduction

As I stand near the Old Country Road entrance to the Roosevelt Field Mall and watch the steady, endless stream of cars enter and exit this busy shopping center, I can hardly believe that I am on the very spot where Charles Lindbergh's famous airplane, the *Spirit of St. Louis*, was stored in a hangar while awaiting its historic flight in May of 1927.

Looking around at the sea of vehicles in the massive parking lot, it's almost inconceivable to think that this was once the country's premier airport, born at a time when this area was the very cradle of the nation's aviation, and growing quickly in the years that followed. Where today shoppers flock, crowds used to come back then, too. But in those days, they gathered to watch daredevils take off or long-distance flight records get broken, not to get candles and sandals.

Early Days

The first flights near what would become Roosevelt Field took place in July 1909, when aviation pioneer Glenn A. Curtiss, who came to Long Island from upstate New York, found the Hempstead Plains to be the ideal location for flying. After all, being the largest prairie east of the Mississippi River meant there was lots of open, flat space that was unobstructed by trees or buildings. Curtiss flew his plane the Golden Flyer (aka Gold Bug), from a field near Washington Avenue in Mineola. His arrival kickstarted aviation in the area; the 350-acre Nassau Boulevard Airfield in Garden City opened in 1910 and soon had thirty-one hangars.

Meanwhile, aviators were also using the great open field a little further east (which would become Roosevelt Field) to fly their planes. It was more ideal than the fields to the west because it offered hundreds of acres of unobstructed flying. This land was purchased by the Hempstead Plains Aviation Company and collectively became known as the Hempstead Plains Aerodrome, which began just east of Clinton Road.

Roosevelt Field, which would tout itself on its stationery as "America's Premier Airport Since 1911," had its origins with aviator Alfred Moisant, who started the Moisant Flying

School on the Hempstead Plains on May 1, 1911, with forty-two pupils using seven biplanes and seven monoplanes. Alfred Moisant was the brother of the more famous John Moisant, a popular early aviator who died in an air crash in Louisiana in 1910. The Moisant Aviation School was immediately a sensation. In June 1911, a Moisant monoplane from the school was suspended from the ceiling of Wanamaker's Department Store in Manhattan; the store served as agents for their planes and you could buy one with a 30 hp engine for $4,000. Moisant had an airplane factory on Ninth Avenue in Manhattan and had built sixteen airplanes in just three months in 1911. The school's instructors were all French aviators. The Moisant School is also where Harriet Quimby, the first woman pilot in the United States, learned to fly and received a pilot's license in August 1911. Matilde Moisant, Alfred's sister, also learned to fly at the school and became the second woman to earn a pilot's license. The Nassau Boulevard field closed in the spring of 1912, relocating operations to the more unobstructed and larger 1,200-acre Moisant Field (accounts of the acreage vary). At one point the school offered a free Moisant monoplane (without motor) to the student who "makes the best record for least breakage, quickness in learning and general aptitude for flying" by May 15, 1913.

The Moisant School only lasted a few years at this location; there are no references to it on Long Island after 1914. Aviation continued on the site; in July 1916, the Signal U.S. Army Corps founded the Signal Corps Aviation Station at the Hempstead Plains Airfield to train pilots in the National Guard. Among those training there was Quentin Roosevelt, son of the former president. Once the United States entered World War I in 1917, the field became focused on training pilots and other airplane crew members for the war effort.

Wartime

In 1917, the Mineola Aviation Field was renamed after Second Lieutenant L. W. Hazelhurst, who had died in an aircraft accident in Maryland in 1912 (although the name Mineola Aviation Field and Aviation Field at Mineola continued to be used as well for a time). Hazelhurst Field (aka Hazelhurst Field #1; Hazelhurst #2 to the southeast was to become Mitchel Field) was hopping with activity during World War I. Aviation would be an important part of the war, and training pilots was critical to a successful wartime aviation effort. Once the United States entered the war in 1917, numerous buildings and other infrastructure were quickly erected to serve the military aviators in training.

Hundreds of planes flew every week, and the local skies were busy with the sights and sounds of these flying (and fighting) machines. Thanks to the very comprehensive efforts of the War Department photographers, there are numerous photos available that document the wartime activities at Hazelhurst. In January 1918, the U.S. School of Aviation Medicine began at Hazelhurst Field, studying the effects of flying on pilot physiology using the latest state-of-the-art equipment. The field was renamed again as Roosevelt Field, in honor of Quentin Roosevelt after his death in France in July 1918. Countless airplanes were used in training the soldiers at the field; there were inevitably several crashes, some of the fatal. Once the war was over, the field returned to civilian flights again.

Curtiss Field vs. Roosevelt Field

On December 27, 1917, the Garden City Company sold Curtiss Engineering Company twenty acres of land at the corner of Clinton and Stewart Avenues. The Curtiss-Wright aircraft factory and testing facility was completed in 1918/19 and began to manufacture airplanes. The Curtiss plant remained in operation until 1932 and in 1940 the building complex was leased to the Sperry Gyroscope Company. The Curtiss factory utilized the western airfield at the corner of Clinton and Old Country Road to test and fly their planes. In September 1919, Roland Rohls, a test pilot for the Curtiss company, set a new world altitude flying record when his plane took off from Roosevelt Field and climbed to 34,610 feet in seventy-eight minutes. By 1921, the western field became known as Curtiss Field.

Technically, what is popularly known as Roosevelt Field now was for about eight years actually three fields: there was Curtiss Field, aka Field No. 1, at the far western end, which is where most of the hangars and infrastructure were located. This was also the location of the original Hazelhurst Field. There was also Old Roosevelt Field, aka Field No 2, which later became the Roosevelt Raceway, and there was a strip of land between the two fields. Though Lindbergh's plane was kept in a hangar at Curtiss Field, he took off from a runway on Roosevelt Field. Still, even at the time, the collective airport was often referred to as Roosevelt Field.

In 1929, Roosevelt Field, Inc. purchased Curtiss Field and consolidated the three into one. In 1936, the eastern portion was sold and first was used for the Vanderbilt Cup Race in 1936, but eventually became home to the Roosevelt Raceway, a harness horse racing track that closed in 1988.

Interestingly, through its existence, Roosevelt Field was considered to be in Mineola (perhaps due to Mineola being the nearest train station and post office at the time), but today the area that used to comprise the airfield is technically Garden City and Westbury—not one part of what was once Roosevelt Field actually falls geographically into what is now considered Mineola.

Transatlantic Flights

As the 1920s progressed, technology kept improving and airplane designs grew more sophisticated. They were more durable and could fly faster than ever before. It would soon be feasible to make the ocean crossing non-stop. Roosevelt Field's reputation as a premier airport grew as the years passed. And it was about to grow from a locally famous airfield to an internationally famous place that would live forever in the history books.

It started in 1926, when a $25,000 prize was offered by New York City hotelier, Raymond Orteig, for the first non-stop flight across the Atlantic between New York and Paris. The first challenger to attempt it was a French World War I flying ace named Captain Rene Fonck, who took off in a Sikorsky model S-26 from Roosevelt Field on September 21, 1926. The plane crashed on takeoff, killing the plane's radio operator. Another who wished to attempt the transatlantic flight was Naval officer and explorer Richard Byrd. In April 1927, he flew a test run of the *America*, a tri-motor Fokker plane, but the plane crashed at Teterboro Airport in

New Jersey, wrecking its nose and central propeller, and injuring Byrd. The *Amerika* arrived at Roosevelt field on May 12, repaired and almost ready to go, but Byrd's wrist was not yet healed so he had to wait. Also in the running was an aviator named Clarence Chamberlain, who had just set a new flying endurance record but who was embroiled in a legal dispute that prevented him from flying in May.

An airmail pilot from the Midwest named Charles Lindbergh was interested in accomplishing this feat. His monoplane, the *Spirit of St. Louis*, had flown for the first time on April 28, and he headed for Roosevelt Field on May 10. But unlike his competition, Lindbergh intended to fly solo. While Byrd's plane waited at Roosevelt Field, Lindbergh's and Chamberlain's planes were nearby at neighboring Curtiss Field.

It was Lindbergh who was ready first. On the morning of May 20, he set off for Roosevelt Field from his room at the Garden City Hotel. A crowd was gathered there to see him off, including Byrd, who wished him well. Lindbergh started down the runway heading east at 7:52 am, his plane just barely clearing a tractor and telephone wires. He was off! After 33½ hours flying, the *Spirit of St. Louis* touched down in Paris. Lindbergh was an immediate cultural icon and forever remained a hero for the rest of his life, and Roosevelt Field's place in history was cemented.

Meanwhile, Chamberlain's legal issues cleared up and he was ready to go on June 4, 1927. He became the second to fly across the Atlantic, the first with a passenger—his backer Charles Levine. His plane landed in Germany after nearly forty-six hours, setting a new endurance record.

Byrd was still not quite ready to fly by the time Lindbergh made a triumphant return to Roosevelt Field on the afternoon of June 16, 1927, after a day of appearances in New York City. Escorted by police on motorcycles and followed by reporters, Lindbergh was greeted by a crowd of 25,000 people. He gave a speech about the importance of building new airports, and then left to cheers.

On June 29, 1927, Byrd and three crew members finally took off from Roosevelt Field, carrying, among other mementos, the silk flag that he'd brought with him when he flew over the North Pole in 1926. They made a water landing upon arrival in France after forty-four hours, but everyone was safe.

In the years to come, there would be other transatlantic flights to follow, and many other record-breaking long-distance flights. In 1930 alone, there were non-stop flights made from Roosevelt Field to Havana, Mexico City, and Ireland. In 1931, Wiley Post and Harold Gatty became the first people to fly around the world in an epic flight that began at Roosevelt Field. In 1932, James Mollison landed at Roosevelt Field after becoming the first to fly solo east-to-west across the Atlantic.

Golden Years

Roosevelt Field was at its peak of popularity in the early 1930s. An expansion program gave it even greater capacity. As a 1932 advertisement boasted, Roosevelt Field had twice as many airplanes than any other metropolitan airport, with fifty buildings and 350,000 square feet of hangar space, including 131,000 square feet of recently constructed steel and concrete hangars. "Use Roosevelt Field" the ad proclaimed: "America's Premier Airport" and "The Center of Commercial Aviation in the East." The field even had an aviation museum that had several airplane engines on display as well as complete pre-1918 airplanes. With one record-breaking flight after another, the field continued to draw the most famous names in worldwide aviation, including Amelia Earhart.

In 1933, the National Charity Air Pageant (to raise money for Depression victims) was held at Roosevelt Field, a two-day event chaired by Eleanor Roosevelt and which drew tens of thousands of people per day; one feature was the destruction of a *papier-mache* "Depressionville" village by bombers from Langley Field, Virginia. The future Pope Pius XII stopped at the field in 1936 before embarking on a tour of the United States. In 1938, Douglas Corrigan flew from California to Roosevelt Field in twenty-seven hours in an old Curtiss airplane. This was an achievement, but he was to become famous for his flight back to California—which he didn't actually make, flying (from nearby Floyd Bennett Field in Brooklyn) to Ireland by mistake and earning him the nickname "Wrong Way" Corrigan.

A popular spot for food and socializing (and overnight stays) was the Roosevelt Field Inn, situated in a building at the northwest corner of the field. It billed itself *circa* 1940 as "the popular rendezvous of the Epicure, meeting place of famous flying folk."

Flying lessons were a big part of what went on at Roosevelt Field. The Roosevelt Aviation School was widely recognized as one of the nation's best. There were also independent flight instructors at the field. In the early 1930s, for example, Allen Hull was offering flying lessons in the recently debuted small and lightweight Taylor Cub airplane. You could learn to fly for $60 and solo flying time was $7.50 an hour—which was a lot for back then, during the Great Depression.

World War II and Decline

With the arrival of World War II, civilian flying stopped at the flying field and it was transitioned into a center for military flight operations. Once the war ended, though, the airport had a hard time recovering its past glory. Civilian flights never reached pre-war levels again. The glory of the 1930s was over. It was the beginning of the end for the storied airfield. In 1949, the Roosevelt Aviation School closed, and the Roosevelt Field Inn declared bankruptcy.

There were many other factors that led to Roosevelt Field's demise, though. Airplanes were getting bigger and faster for one, and outgrowing fields such as Roosevelt Field. At 500 acres in the early 1930s, it was cut in half by the removal of the eastern portion which became Roosevelt Raceway. Other airports of the 1940s were much larger—LaGuardia (opened 1939) at 680 acres and Idlewild (the future JFK, opened in 1948) at several thousand acres. Not only that, those two airports were located within the city limits of New York, making them preferable for people in and near the city. And besides, the suburbs around Roosevelt Field were growing. More houses and people, especially just to the north of Old Country Road, made an airport in their midst less favorable. It was too noisy and dangerous to have planes taking off and landing in this area.

In 1950 Roosevelt Field was sold, and on May 31, 1951, the runways were officially closed. The famous Hangar Number 16 where Lindbergh's had been stored before his historic flight was demolished in October 1951 and with it the hopes of preserving anything of the legacy of the world's most famous flight. The western portion of the field was developed soon after and the Roosevelt Field Mall was opened in 1956. The northernmost section of the Meadowbrook Parkway was also built in the mid-1950s, cutting right through the former airfield. There were still a few hangars left until 1973 and then that was all. The last visible traces of what had once been the world's most famous airport were gone. The airfield had been replaced with parking fields and the retail establishments that went with them. Roosevelt Raceway continued to operate for almost forty years after Roosevelt Field closed, and then it too was shuttered and eventually demolished, leaving nothing intact from the era of the world's premier airport.

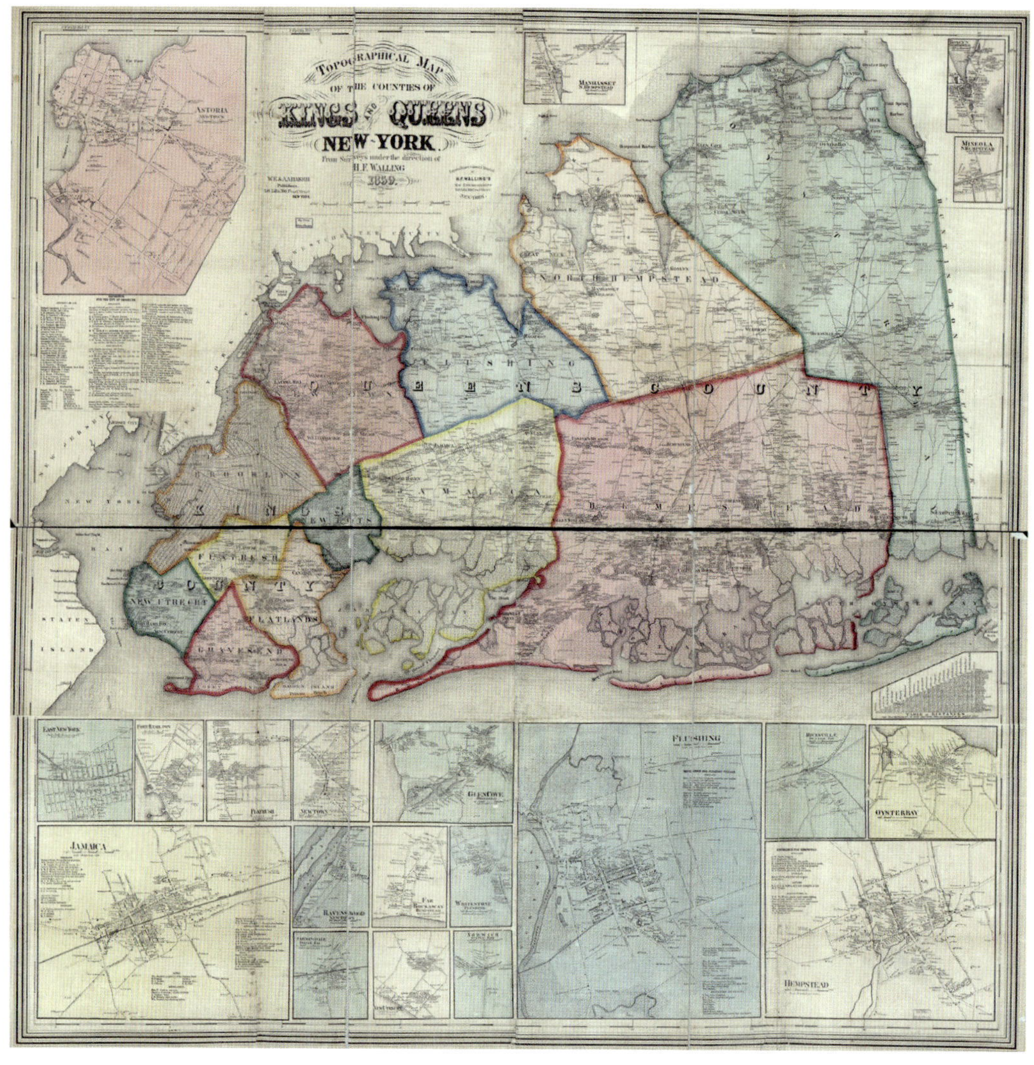

An 1859 map shows the area of the Hempstead Plains southeast of Mineola and northeast of Hempstead, that was to become Roosevelt Field—roughly between the O and the U in the word County.

The Herring-Curtiss *Golden Flyer*, flown by aviation pioneer Glenn Curtiss at Mineola in 1909. It was Curtiss selecting this area on the Hempstead Plains as ideal for flying who sparked the birth of Long Island as the Cradle of Aviation. The bottom image shows a crowd on a field around Curtiss and his airplane.

FARMAN BIPLANE
CURTIS BIPLANE

Aviator Paul Peck in a helicopter designed by Berliner in Mineola, *circa* 1911.

OPPOSITE PAGE:

Above: This *circa* 1910 image shows a Curtiss biplane and a Farman biplane in the air at the Mineola Aviation Field. The Farman plane, a French aircraft, was first built in 1909 by the Farman Aviation Works. It was flown at Mineola in 1910 by an English aviator named Claude Grahame-White.

Below: In October 1910, aviator Charles Keeney Hamilton made three circles in the air at the flying field near Hempstead with his 110 hp airplane. When he took off, he sent hats flying into the air, according to a newspaper account of the time. This photograph shows Hamilton with a crowd after his flight.

In 1911, Harriet Quimby became the first licensed female pilot in the United States. She had taken flying lessons at the newly formed Moisant Aviation School on the Hempstead Plains (on the site of what would become Roosevelt Field), with a two-and-a-half-mile long course on ten square miles of open land. Quimby would die in a tragic flying accident in 1912.

Right: An advertisement for the Moisant Aviation School in a 1912 issue of an aviation magazine. Aviation on Long Island began in the Garden City/Mineola/Westbury area and continued to be a presence there until the closure of Mitchel Field (originally known as Aviation Field #2 or Hazelhurst Field #2) in 1961.

Below: Earl Ovington piloted the first airmail flight in the country on September 26, 1911. He took off from the Nassau Boulevard Aerodrome in Garden City carrying a bag of mail that he dropped over Mineola (not far from the future site of Roosevelt Field). Ovington is seated in his Bleriot airplane; also in the photo are Frank Harris Hitchcock, postmaster general, and Edward M. Morgan, postmaster of New York.

Close-up of cockpits of Bleriot-type airplane (aka an imitation of the real thing, which was a French machine) built by the American Aeroplane Supply House, on Franklin Street in Hempstead, 1912. Planes built here flew at the nearby flying field to the north that would eventually become Roosevelt Field.

The American Aeroplane Supply House at 266-268 Franklin Street, Hempstead, manufactured replicas of Bleriot-type monoplanes (and unabashedly advertised that fact). On June 30, 1911, Willie Haupt made a twelve-minute flight at an altitude of 500 feet at the Mineola Aviation Field in one of their machines. The image here dates to 1912 and shows one of their Bleriot-type planes at Garden City.

This photo from June 10, 1913, shows noted aviator Clyde Murvin Wood flying over the International Polo Tournament at the Meadowbrook Club, which was just southeast of where Roosevelt Field would soon be located.

The polo field of the Meadowbrook Club (also known as Meadow Brook), adjacent to what was to become Roosevelt Field, seen during an international match in June 1913.

Flying Together, Aviation Field, L. I.

A postcard *circa* late 1910s from the Aviation Field at Mineola shows a biplane and an American flag. The flag appears to be the twenty-five-star flag which dates to between 1896-1908.

An army airplane flies over a then-makeshift encampment at the Aviation Field at Mineola, *circa* 1916 or early 1917.

Army officers observing students on test flights in one of the first photos taken with government permission at the Army Aviation School after American joined World War I in 1917.

An early wreck at the army Aviation Field, on May 7, 1917, of a plane flown by Ransom Merritt and Anthony Spileno. The *New York Times* headline regarding this bizarre and tragic story read: NOVICE AIRMEN DIE IN 1,500-FOOT PLUNGE; Two Army Pupils Take Plane at Mineola Without Authority and Attempt Flight. THEY SOON LOSE CONTROL Crowd Sees Runaway Biplane Zigzag Dizzily in the Sky, Then Drop to Earth.

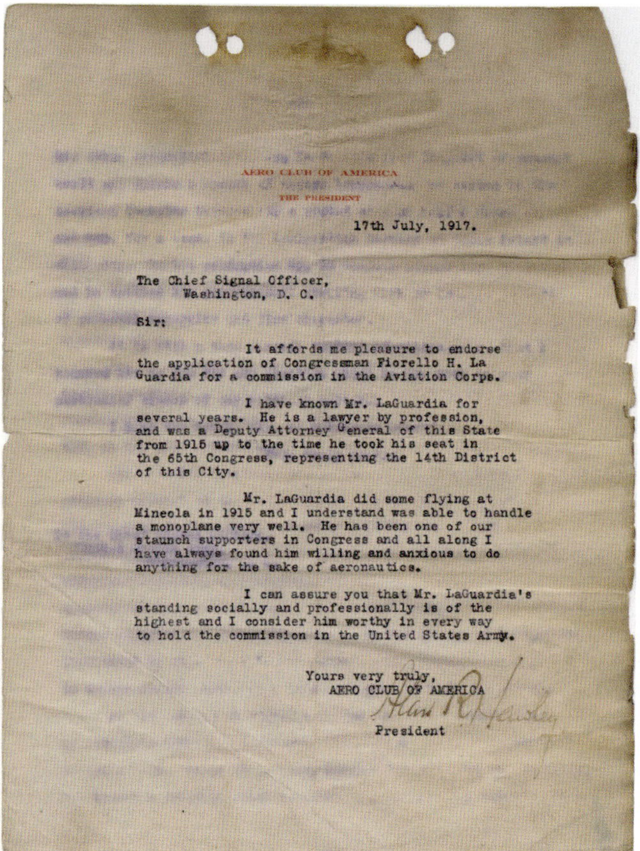

AERO CLUB OF AMERICA

THE PRESIDENT

17th July, 1917.

The Chief Signal Officer,
Washington, D. C.

Sir:

It affords me pleasure to endorse the application of Congressman Fiorello H. La Guardia for a commission in the Aviation Corps.

I have known Mr. LaGuardia for several years. He is a lawyer by profession, and was a Deputy Attorney General of this State from 1915 up to the time he took his seat in the 65th Congress, representing the 14th District of this City.

Mr. LaGuardia did some flying at Mineola in 1915 and I understand was able to handle a monoplane very well. He has been one of our staunch supporters in Congress and all along I have always found him willing and anxious to do anything for the sake of aeronautics.

I can assure you that Mr. LaGuardia's standing socially and professionally is of the highest and I consider him worthy in every way to hold the commission in the United States Army.

Yours very truly,
AERO CLUB OF AMERICA

President

Above: A lineup of army aviators at the Aviation Field decked out in their leather jackets, June 1917.

Left: A letter of recommendation for then Congressman and future New York City mayor, Fiorello LaGuardia, from the Aero Club of America dated July 17, 1917, states that Mr. LaGuardia had flying experience at the aviation field in Mineola in 1915.

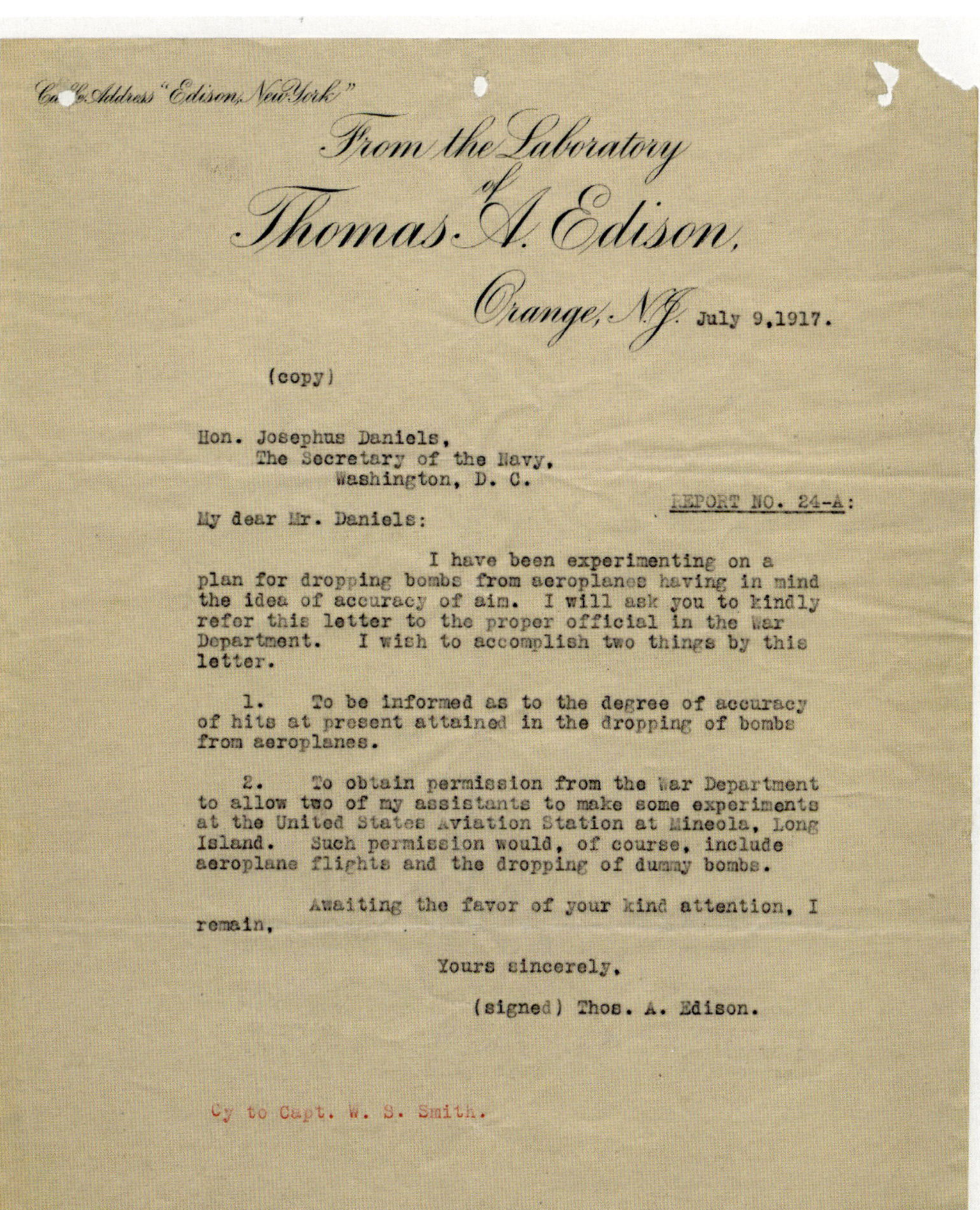

Cable Address "Edison, New York"

From the Laboratory of Thomas A. Edison, Orange, N.J. July 9, 1917.

(copy)

Hon. Josephus Daniels,
The Secretary of the Navy,
Washington, D. C.

REPORT NO. 24-A:

My dear Mr. Daniels:

I have been experimenting on a plan for dropping bombs from aeroplanes having in mind the idea of accuracy of aim. I will ask you to kindly refer this letter to the proper official in the War Department. I wish to accomplish two things by this letter.

1. To be informed as to the degree of accuracy of hits at present attained in the dropping of bombs from aeroplanes.

2. To obtain permission from the War Department to allow two of my assistants to make some experiments at the United States Aviation Station at Mineola, Long Island. Such permission would, of course, include aeroplane flights and the dropping of dummy bombs.

Awaiting the favor of your kind attention, I remain,

Yours sincerely,

(signed) Thos. A. Edison.

Cy to Capt. W. S. Smith.

A letter from Thomas Edison to the Secretary of War in July 1917, asking if his assistants could perform some experiments at the Aviation Field relating to targeting accuracy of dropping bombs from airplanes.

A wrecked airplane at the Mineola Aviation Field, July 1917. There were countless plane wrecks at the site of Roosevelt Field over the years, and many deaths and injuries as a result, especially in the early years when plane technology was still in its infancy.

From left to right: Captain Boynein, Lieutenant Tabuatien of the French Aero Corps, and at center, Lieutenant General Roop of Russia, who was in the United States with the Russian Mission, in a photo taken at the Mineola Aviation Field on July 14, 1917.

Visiting French aviators and their hosts at the Aviation Field in July 1917.

Aviation lineup at muster on July 31, 1917, at the Aviation Field in Mineola.

Men and horses clearing pre-winter snow from a runway at Hazelhurst Field on November 6, 1917.

Once Hazelhurst Field, the military airfield, became Curtiss/Roosevelt Field, the civilian airfield, the building infrastructure was updated, and it looked completely different than what you can see in this image.

Above: United States Marine Corps officers Albert Sidney McLemore (1869-1921), head of recruitment; Captain Thomas G. Sterrett, head of the Publicity Bureau and others on the set of a World War I recruitment film made by the Edison Company in Mineola, New York in 1917.

Right: A man stationed in the observation tower at the Aviation Field in December 1917, observing the flights of army aviators on a day when the temperature was 3 degrees Fahrenheit.

Hangars and Curtiss training airplanes at Hazelhurst Field in February 1918 in a photo taken by the U.S. School of Military Cinematography of Columbia University.

W.O. 932
A-1173

SIGNAL CORPS MOTION PICTURE LABORATORY
WASHINGTON BARRACKS
WASHINGTON, D.C.

March 6, 1918.

From Signal Corps Motion Picture Laboratory
Washington Barracks, Washington, D. C.

To Acting Director, War Plans Division
War College, Washington, D. C.

C5070-C5098

Subject Censoring Motion Picture Positive.

1. Transmitted herewith motion picture positive, subject No. 26.

Title: ACTIVITIES AT HAZLEHURST FIELD 1135 feet.

Photographed By: Privates Guetlein & Downs (School of Mil. Cine.)

At: Hazlehurst Field, Mineola, Long Island.

Date: February 18, 1918.

Description:

Trucks exit from garage. Means of transportation.
Assembling motors.
Unloading airplane from freight car to truck.
Planes pass camera on ground.
Inspection of plane before flight.
Group of officers.
Captain Thomas Hitchcock.
Review of entire personnel marching.
Captain Hitchcock getting in plane.
Plane's rudder tested.
Plane taxing.
Plane coming up to start and leaving.
Soldiers in column of squads marching.

R. J. Holman
1st Lieut. Sig. R. C.
Motion Picture Lab.

1st Ind.

Acting Director, War Plans Division, War College, Washington, March 6, 1918.
To Signal Corps Motion Picture Laboratory, Washington Barracks, D. C.

Returned.
1. The above subject is released.

D. W. KETCHAM
Colonel, General Staff
Acting Director, War Plans Division
Acting Assistant Chief of Staff

By John R M Jaeger
Maj. USA. Historical Branch War Plans Division

A memo dated March 6, 1918, from the Signal Corps Motion Picture Laboratory about film footage taken at Hazelhurst Field for use in an Army film reel about war training activities. The memo details which scenes were shot.

A lineup of fifteen airplanes at Hazelhurst Field #1, which would later be renamed Roosevelt Field, waiting to fly for the Second Liberty Loan in March 1918.

Flying cadets inspecting a French Nieuport airplane at Hazelhurst Field in March 1918, in front of Hangar No. 26.

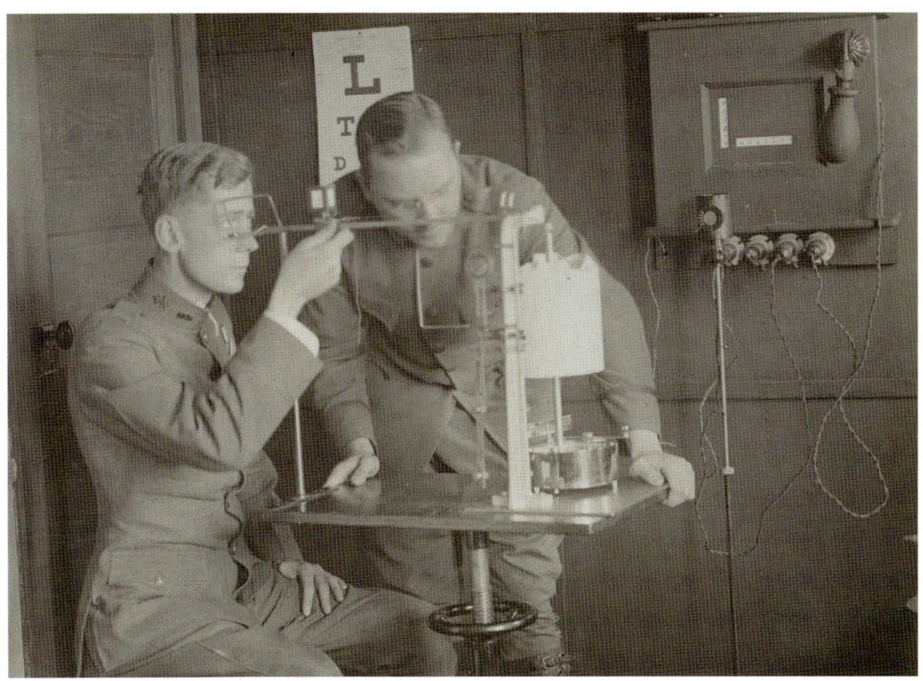

Howe's Ophthalmic Ergograph at the Medical Research Laboratory was used for testing the eyes' accommodation under reduced oxygen levels, as seen in a March 15, 1918, photograph.

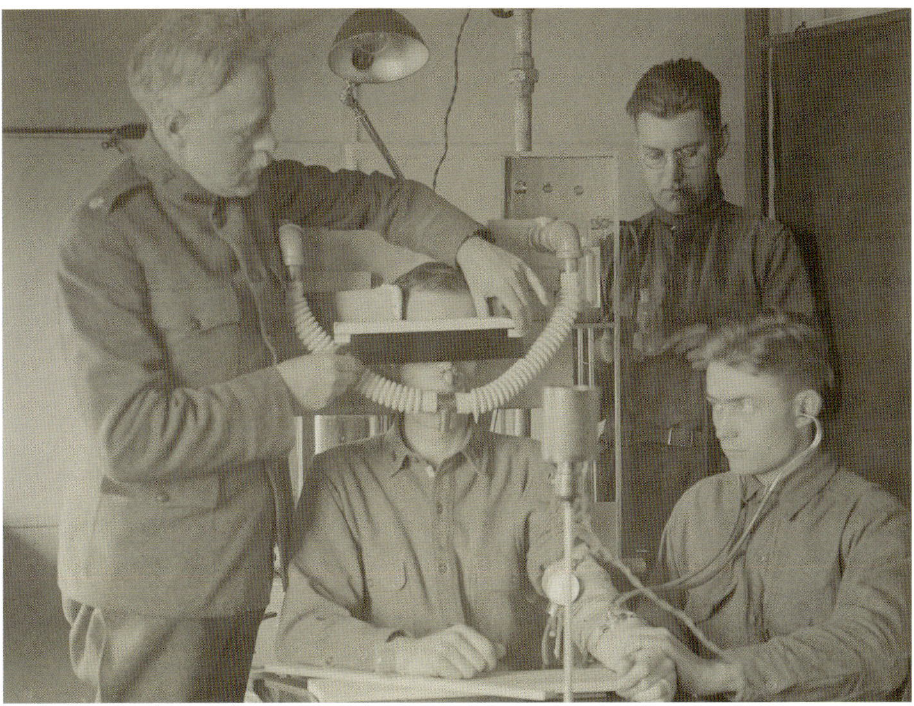

Testing retinal sensitivity on March 15, 1918, at the Medical Research Laboratory at Hazelhurst, something useful for aviators working at night.

This Low Pressure Tank at the Medical Research Laboratory at Hazelhurst Field (photographed March 18, 1918) was used to test oxygen want at the same time as reduced atmospheric pressure.

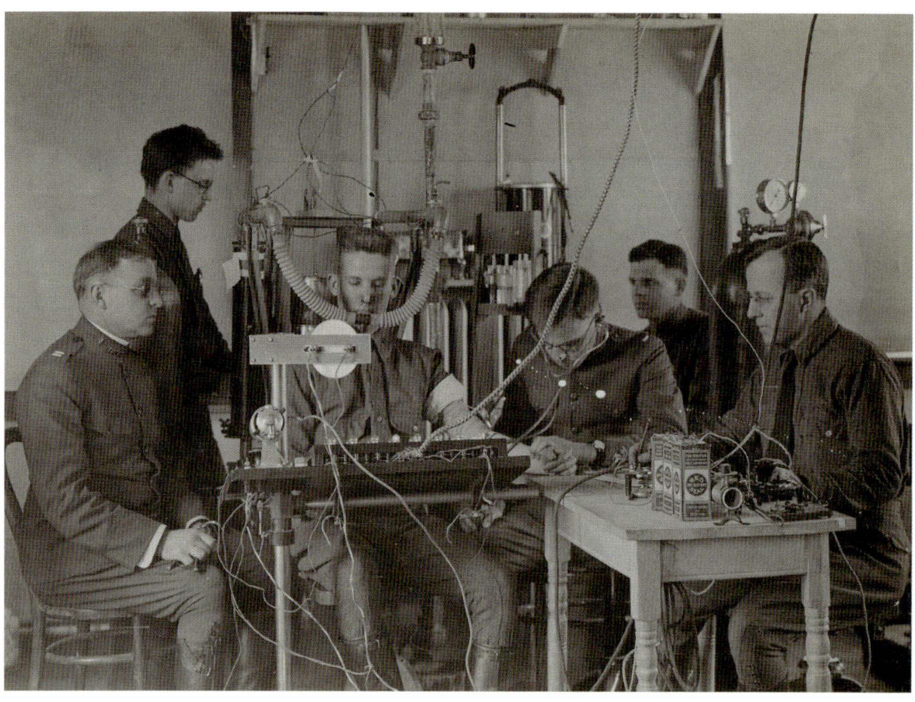

This photo taken at the Medical Research Laboratory on March 18, 1918, shows apparatus for volition and attention tests under low oxygen conditions that an aviator was going to encounter.

The Army established the Medical Research Laboratory at Hazelhurst Field, in Mineola, New York, in January 1918, to study flight effects on the human body. This photo from March 18, 1918, shows the staff of the laboratory in front of the building.

A group of officers at Hazelhurst Field, April 25, 1918, with Major E. L. Canady as their commanding officer. The building they are standing in front of, like all the others at the field, was likely constructed very recently to accommodate the field's use by the army after the United States' entry into World War I.

On April 26, 1918, Major George Tulasne, chief of the French aviation mission to the United States, and Lieutenant George Flachaire, flew from the Mineola Aviation Field to Washington, D.C., stopped there for lunch, and returned to New York in time for dinner. The 500-mile round trip was said to be a record for cross-country flying at the time.

Opposite page:

Captain Antonion Silvio Resnati, an Italian aviator, died at Hazelhurst Field in May 1918 when the Caproni plane he was test flying nose-dived to the ground from 100 feet in the air. The top photo shows Major E. L. Canady in a Caproni biplane flying over Fifth Avenue, New York, during Resnati's funeral on May 22, 1918. The bottom image shows a funeral procession moving up Fifth Avenue; the Caproni is visible in this photo as well.

BUILD
MUTUAL TOBAC
TOBACCO
JEWELE
GAGE E. TA

Side view of a wrecked Spad airplane at Hazelhurst Field, June 6, 1918. This plane escaped more serious damage; a collapsed right front wheel is evident.

Opposite page:

Above: A large three-motor Caproni biplane, carrying seven people, took off from Hazelhurst Field and flew over a crowd at the Gymkhana held in June 1918 on Captain John S. Phipps' polo field in what is now known as Old Westbury. Leaflets can be seen dropping from the plane.

Below: A closer look at the Caproni flying over the Phipps polo field in June 1918. The Phipps estate is today Old Westbury Gardens.

Kirkham Triplane manufactured by the Curtiss Engineering Corp., Garden City, Long Island. Side view and front view of plane in field (possibly Curtiss Field), July 6, 1918.

Captain Joseph D'Annunzio, son of the celebrated Italian poet and aviator, standing with Guiliuno Carvese, who piloted the first American-built Caproni C-45 when it was officially tested at Hazelhurst Field, in a photo taken on September 26, 1918.

Making preparations on the new three-engine Liberty Caproni CA-5 bombing plane, prior to a demonstration flight at Hazelhurst Field in September 1918.

Side view of the Caproni CA-5 just before its demonstration flight in September 1918.

The Caproni CA-5 on its test flight in 1918.

Getting out of airplanes was no easy task, as shown in this photo of a passenger stepping down from a Caproni CA-5.

Captain Hugo D'Annunzio, son of Gabrielle D'Annunzio, famous Italian aviator and poet, inspects the new Liberty Caproni CA-5 before a demonstration at Hazelhurst Field in September 1918.

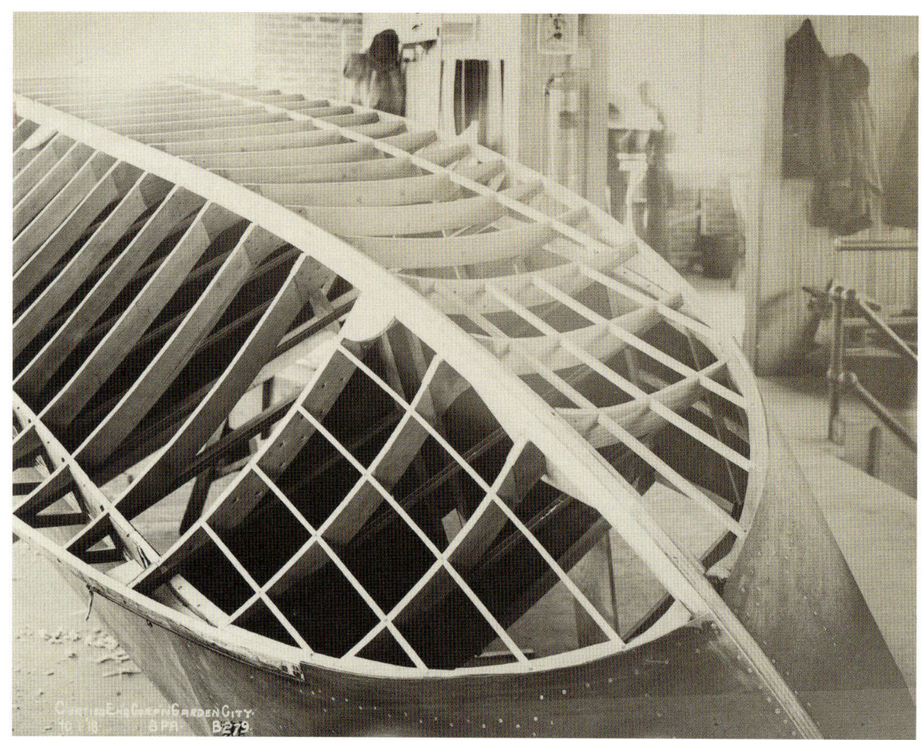

A type M. F. Curtiss Flying Boat, aka hydroplane, under construction at the factory on Clinton Road, in a photo taken on October 1, 1918. In December 1917, the Garden City Company sold the Curtiss Engineering Company 20 acres at the corner of Clinton and Stewart Avenues. On this plot of land, Glenn Curtiss had an airplane research and manufacturing facility built.

The NC-1, the world's largest flying boat, built by the Curtiss company in Garden City in a photo dated November 26, 1918. This airplane and three others like it set off to try to become the first planes to fly across the Atlantic. One did make it, the NC-4.

Circa 1918 photos show airplanes in battle formation in the sky above Hazelhurst Field.

Close-up views of military airplanes in a training flight in the sky over Hazelhurst Field *circa* 1918.

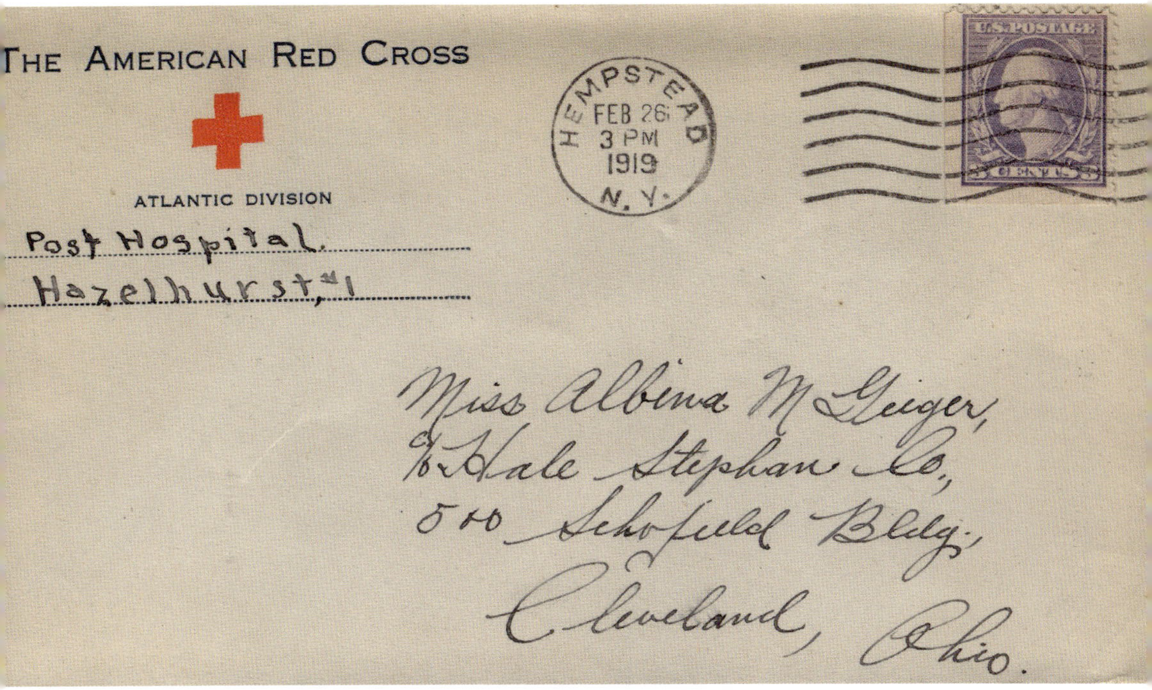

THE AMERICAN RED CROSS

ATLANTIC DIVISION

Post Hospital.
Hazelhurst #1

HEMPSTEAD FEB 26 3 PM 1919 N.Y.

U.S. POSTAGE 3 CENTS 3

Miss Albina M. Geiger,
c/o Hale Stephan Co.,
500 Schofield Bldg.,
Cleveland, Ohio.

An envelope sent from the Post Hospital at Hazelhurst Field #1 in February 1919. By this time, the field had been renamed to Roosevelt Field, but the old name apparently still lingered.

A naval kite balloon used as a marker in July 1919, in case of clouds—it was sent above cloud level to give the British R-34 airship a landmark to make landing at Roosevelt Field easier after its record-setting transatlantic flight. The Navy had Roosevelt Field surrounded by powerful searchlights which illuminated the field at night in preparation for the arrival of the R-34.

Hydrogen gas supplies awaiting the British airship R-34 at Roosevelt Field in July 1919.

A view of the British coat of arms on the nose of the British dirigible R-34, which arrived after a transatlantic flight from England at Roosevelt Field on July 6, 1919.

The two center gondolas of the R-34 both had an engine and a propeller.

This image captures the impressive full length of the R-34 dirigible at Roosevelt Field in July 1919, not long before it made its return trip to England.

In an official Navy Test, this Curtiss Triplane established a new world record in September 1919 for speed and climbing. Fully loaded and equipped, this plane achieved the speed of 160 miles an hour and climbed 12,500 feet in ten minutes. The machine was equipped with a Curtiss Type, model K 12-cylinder engine, capable of attaining 400 hp. The photo shows it at the plant of the Curtiss Engineering Corporation.

Archie Miller, Emil Kiel, and Frank McKee at Roosevelt Field, Long Island, after they landed during the Transcontinental Aerial Derby between Roosevelt Field and San Francisco in October 1919.

Emmett Tanner, Carl "Tooey" Spatz (later changed to Spaatz), and Archie Miller at Roosevelt Field, Long Island, after they landed during the Transcontinental Aerial Derby in October 1919, with Spatz's family.

This photograph shows aviators who participated in the October 1919 Transcontinental Aerial Derby (aka the transcontinental reliability and endurance test): Captain Guy De Lavergne, Colonel Archie Miller, Major Langlois, and General William Mitchell.

COL. ARCHIE MILLER - BENEDICT CROWELL - LT. ROSS KIRKPATRICK - GEN. WM. MITCHELL

Lieutenant W. R. Taylor in the air at the 1919 transcontinental reliability and endurance test between Mineola, New York, and San Francisco. The airplane he is flying is the *Ansaldo SVA* (named for Savoia-Verduzio-Ansaldo), an Italian reconnaissance biplane.

Opposite page:

Above: This photo shows Colonel Archie Miller, First Assistant Secretary of War Benedict Crowell, Lieutenant Ross Kirkpatrick, General William Mitchell, Sergeant E. N. Bruce before an ill-fated flight for the Transcontinental Aerial Derby. Once Crowell and the pilot were airborne, the engine died, and the plane stalled and crashed. Emerging from the wreckage, Crowell said: "That's the shortest flight on record. I'd go up again right now if I didn't have an appointment which I must keep in the city."

Below: William E. Kline, a dog named "Trixie" and Lieutenant B. W. Maynard about to embark (no pun intended) on the transcontinental flight in 1919.

A Russian immigrant named Igor Sikorsky started building airplanes in Westbury during the early 1920s, with financial aid from fellow Russian, the famous pianist Sergei Rachmaninoff. In May 1924, a large Sikorsky biplane took off on a test flight from Roosevelt Field. The plane, carrying nine people, crash-landed on the nearby Salisbury Golf Course (no serious injuries). Sikorsky perfected this plane, capable of carrying twenty passengers, and it was soon making flights of several hundred miles. By the end of 1926, the plane, called the *Yorktown*, had made its 500th flight and carried over 4,000 passengers. Photo at top shows a Sikorsky S29A plane, made at the factory in Westbury, mid-1920s, and at bottom a closeup of the Sikorsky S29A, showing the marking.

Opposite above: A view of the Curtiss Manufacturing Company taken on April 28, 1925, looking north. The road at left is Clinton Road. The bridge at top is part of the Long Island Motor Parkway.

Joseph Lannin (right), seen here at a Boston Red Sox baseball game at Fenway Park *circa* 1916, was not only owner of the Red Sox, he also owned Roosevelt Field during the 1920s through his Lannin Realty Company, until his death in 1928. He also owned the adjacent Salisbury Golf Club (later to become Eisenhower Park).

Captain Rene Fonck's Sikorsky airplane in flames after it crashed at Roosevelt Field on September 21, 1926, during Fonck's attempt to become the first to fly across the Atlantic, months before Lindbergh actually accomplished it. The radio operator and mechanic were killed in the crash, but Fonck and his alternate pilot escaped.

Transatlantic flight hopeful Commander Richard E. Byrd emerges from a hangar at Roosevelt Field and walks toward his plane, the *America*, May 15, 1927. Byrd had been hoping to become the first across the Atlantic but injured his hand when his plane crashed and was not quite ready in time to make the attempt before Lindbergh.

Above: Charles Lindbergh and his plane at Roosevelt Field just before taking off on his historic flight on May 20, 1927.

Right: An iconic image of Charles Lindbergh in front of his historic plane the *Spirit of St. Louis*.

Left: Charles Lindbergh shaking hands on May 31, 1927 with two others who had been contenders for first to fly across the Atlantic—Clarence Chamberlin (right) and Richard Byrd (center) with the *Spirit of St. Louis* behind them.

Below: Upon his triumphant return to New York after his historic flight, Charles Lindbergh spent four days in the city before heading back to Long Island where he was to take off for St. Louis on June 17, 1927. This photo, taken at neighboring Mitchel Field, shows Lindbergh thanking the police escort that had accompanied him on his New York trip.

Above: Commander Richard Byrd's plane, *America*, shortly after it took off for Europe from Roosevelt Field on June 29, 1927, shortly after 4:30 am. Byrd had three others on board the plane with him. Though Lindbergh had been the first to make that ocean crossing a month earlier, Byrd was not deterred and insisted on making the flight anyway.

Right: Aviator Ruth Elder, seen here with a flashlight at Roosevelt Field in 1927, was the first woman to attempt to fly across the Atlantic Ocean. On October 11, 1927, she set out with fellow aviator George Haldeman, but they fell short when their plane had mechanical issues. She was still greeted with much fanfare on her return to New York.

Lindbergh's historic flight was commemorated in many ways, one of which was a 10-cent postage airmail stamp. But the image has significance beyond the stamp itself; this envelope was carried by Lindbergh on a Contract Airmail Route from Chicago to St. Louis on February 20, 1928, less than a year after he flew across the ocean. He had flown the route previously in 1926 before he became famous, hence the "Lindbergh flies again" wording.

This June 12, 1928, aerial view taken from 800 feet up shows the Curtiss factory complex. The Curtiss Flying Field, used to test its planes, to the northeast of the factory merged with Roosevelt Field.

Ireland Amphiplane

The only plane of its kind in production. Excellently adapted for shuttle work between airports and intown water landings. As supplementary equipment for passenger air lines or for flying services it is the safest, most practical and profitable of commercial aircraft.

Powered with a Wright Whirlwind mounted as a pusher. Cruising speed, 85 miles per hour. Open or closed cockpit—5 place.

Write for complete details.

IRELAND AIRCRAFT, INC.

GARDEN CITY, NEW YORK

A 1928 advertisement for Ireland Aircraft's "Ireland Amphiplane" an amphibious plane, aka seaplane, that was manufactured at their facility at Curtiss/Roosevelt Field. The ad proclaimed it was "the only plane of its kind in production."

Compliments of

Meadow Brook Pharmacy

CHARLES BAUER, Proprietor

SICK ROOM SUPPLIES

"Prescriptions Filled In A Safe, Satisfactory Way"

POST AVENUE **WESTBURY, L. I.**

An April 17, 1929, advertisement for the Meadow Brook Pharmacy on Post Avenue in Westbury, where Charles Lindbergh stopped for ice cream sodas while preparing for his transatlantic flight.

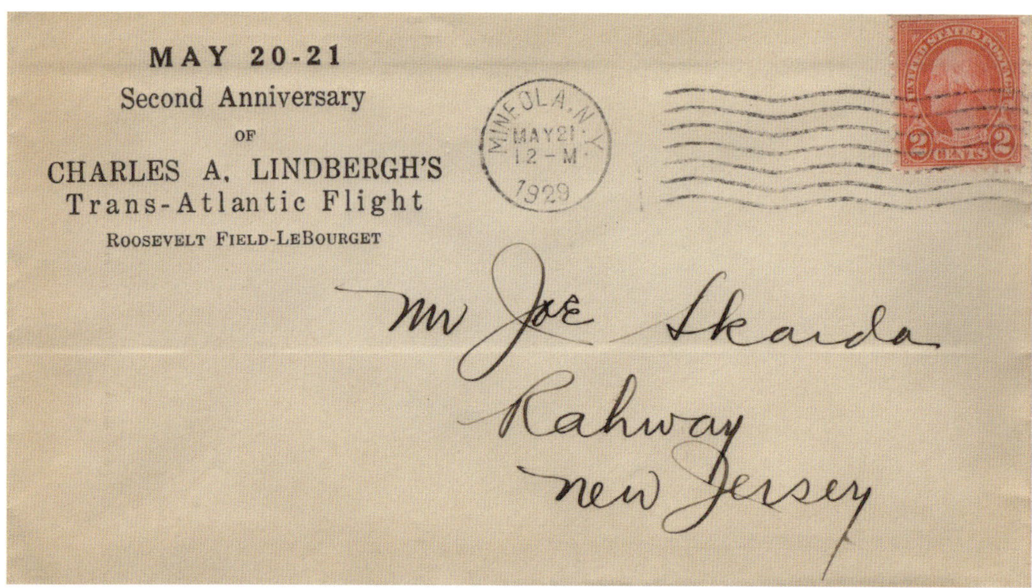

A postal cover commemorating the second anniversary of Lindbergh's transatlantic flight, postmarked May 21, 1929, in Mineola. Celebration and appreciation of this feat began immediately and continues to this day.

Captain Frank Hawks flew from Los Angeles to Roosevelt Field in seventeen hours, thirty-three minutes, and fifty-six seconds (arriving June 29, 1929), which broke his own previous record for a west-east coast-to-coast flight. His Lockheed-Vega plane did not land cleanly, though, striking a fence as it touched down. Hawks was not injured, though the plane was damaged.

Right: A framed snapshot of four aviators at Roosevelt Field in September 1929. The field was used by countless flyers of all skill levels over the years, from casual pilots to record-setting world-famous aviators.

Below: Dieudonne Costes and Maurice Bellonte, two French aviators, flew from Paris to Curtiss/Roosevelt Field on September 1, 1930, becoming the first people to fly an airplane west to east nonstop across the Atlantic. This image on an old French postcard shows them in a parade down Broadway in New York City after their successful flight.

The bottom right of an aerial view of Mineola from 5,000 feet up, taken on April 18, 1931, shows the western edge of Roosevelt Field. A hangar with the word "Roosevelt" on it is visible, as is a building that says "Air Associates," one of the companies with a presence at the air field. The image shows the intersection of Clinton/Glen Cove Road with Old Country Road. This part of Roosevelt Field was formerly Curtiss Field and had recently been incorporated into Roosevelt Field when this photo was taken.

On June 23, 1931, aviators Wiley Post and Harold Gatty took off from Roosevelt Field on what would be the first airplane flight around the world, in Post's plane, *The Winnie Mae*. They landed at Roosevelt Field eight days later, on July 1. These two commemorative covers postmarked July 30, 1931, and August 27, 1931, celebrate Post and Gatty's triumphant visits to Newark, New Jersey, and Los Angeles, California, part of a celebratory trip they took around the United States.

In the summer of 1932, five years after Lindbergh's historic flight, the Scottish pilot Captain James Mollison became the first person to fly solo across the Atlantic Ocean from Europe to America. When his plane *The Hearts Content* touched down at Roosevelt Field on August 21, 1932, he was greeted by a crowd of thousands of people. His plane was a de Haviland Puss Moth model, capable of flying nearly 125 mph.

Mollison flew from Portmarnock Strand, Ireland, to Pennfield Ridge, New Brunswick, Canada, in about thirty hours, and that itself was the historic flight. By the time he continued to Roosevelt Field, he'd already made history. These images show Captain Mollison standing at a table in a hangar with what appears to be some of the pistons from his engine as his plane was tuned up for the return trip back to Europe.

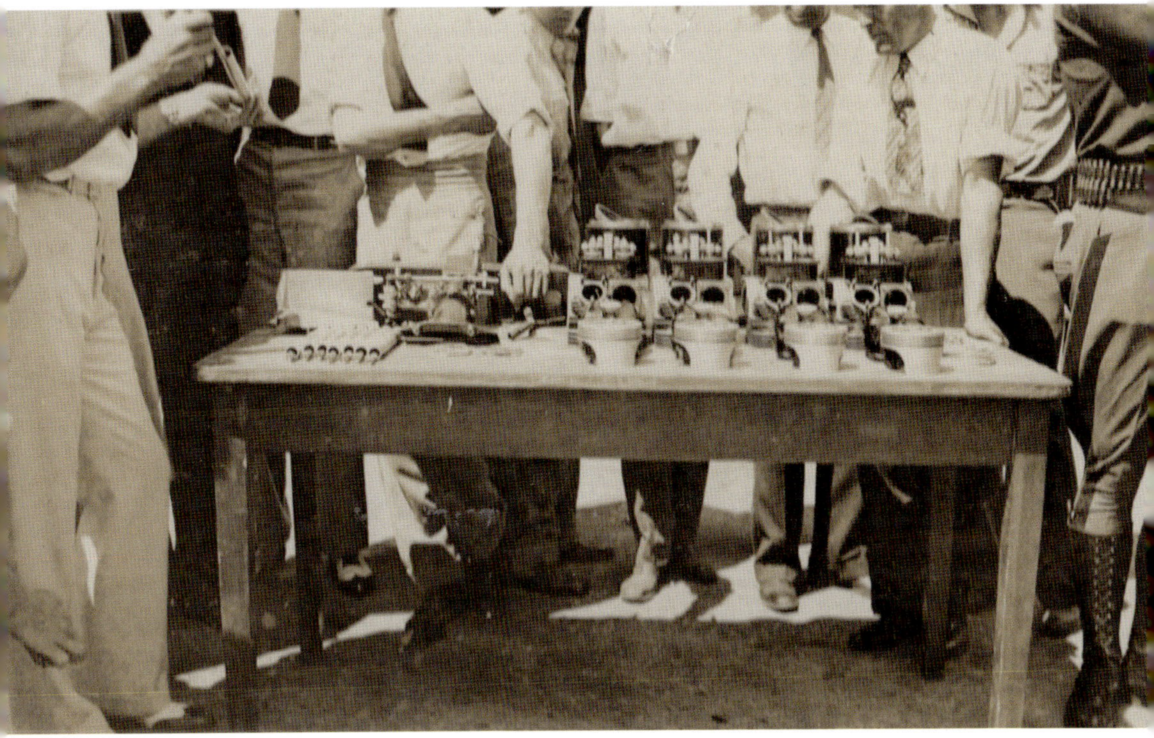

A fire in a Roosevelt Field hangar on June 2, 1933, destroyed eleven airplanes and caused $200,000 of damage. It started with an explosion at the hangar of Engineers Service, Inc. Flames could be seen for miles and attracted spectators who came to witness the conflagration.

Opposite page:

Above: Aero Trades was one of the aviation companies with a long presence at Roosevelt Field. A group of Aero Trades employees stand inside a hangar at Roosevelt Field in 1932.

Below: A *circa* 1932 snapshot of Roosevelt Field captures a great deal: the recently built more modern Art Deco style hangars, parked cars, people walking around, airplanes on the ground, and one in the air. The reverse of the image has a handwritten note that says "Roosevelt Field New Section. We passed this place at night, so you probably won't recognize it."

The presence of a world class airfield drew many airplane manufacturers to the area, including the James V. Martin Airplane Factory, located in Garden City, seen here in two snowy aerial images from February 1934.

This photo shows the famous Wiley Post airplane Winnie Mae being unloaded at Bolling Field, Washington D.C., on December 2, 1935, where it was to be stored in the Smithsonian Institution alongside Lindbergh's plane, the *Spirit of St. Louis*.

Above: A *circa* mid-1930s image of nine people standing in front of a plane at Roosevelt Field. From left: Waldo Fraser, Bill Schaffer, Sadie Hawkins, unknown, unknown, Mr. and Mrs. H. P. Trusty, Trusty's sister, and at far right, Will Trusty.

Right: A *circa* mid-1930s photo of a plane in front of the Aero Trades hangar at Roosevelt Field.

Vintage aerial views of Roosevelt Field are rather elusive, but in this September 1936 view of the Cherry Valley Golf Course in Garden City, the western end of Roosevelt Field is visible; note the airfield hangars in the cropped and zoomed view below, along Clinton Road and Old Country Road.

This 1936 aerial view shows the newly built Roosevelt Raceway, on what used to be the easternmost part of Roosevelt Field. The George Vanderbilt Cup Races were held there in October 1936, the heir to the original Vanderbilt Cup races held by William K. Vanderbilt, Jr. in the early years of the twentieth century. The center right corner of the image also captures the Long Island Motor Parkway's "Roosevelt Field Bridge" which provided access from Stewart Avenue to Roosevelt Field.

This aerial view of the Roosevelt Raceway taken on October 12, 1936, captures the eastern edge of Roosevelt Field. In the cropped image at bottom, several airplanes are clearly visible.

Above: This 1936 photograph was taken outside the Aero Trades hangar at Roosevelt Field. Aero Trades was the company that serviced William K. Vanderbilt's Sikorsky S-43 seaplane, seen here. A group of Aero Trades employees pose in front of the massive aircraft.

Right: In October 1936, future Pope Pius XII, Cardinal Eugenio Pacelli, visited the United States. He is seen here in front of a chartered United Air Lines plane at Roosevelt Field, about to embark on a seven-city U. S. tour with Bishop (future Cardinal) Francis Spellman of New York.

Left: Boy Scouts, officials, and locals gather in May 1937 for the dedication of an official New York State Education Department plaque marking the spot where Charles Lindbergh's plane became airborne ten years earlier.

Below: The luxurious interior cabin of William K. Vanderbilt Jr.'s Sikorsky S-43 airplane in a photo taken on June 10, 1937, at Roosevelt Field. Note the realistic looking clouds painted on the back of the cabin and on the strip surrounding the windows.

ROOSEVELT FIELD INC.

ROOSEVELT AVIATION SCHOOL INC.
ROOSEVELT FLYING CORPORATION

W. D. GUTHRIE, PRESIDENT & TREASURER
A. C. KENNEDY, VICE-PRESIDENT & SECRETARY
W. P. STUCHEL, ASSISTANT TREASURER

America's Premier Airport Since 1911

MINEOLA, L.I., N.Y.
TELEPHONE GARDEN CITY 8000

November 6, 1937

Mr. Alexander Bodnar
1883 Clinton Avenue
Bronx, New York

Dear Mr. Bodnar:

There is a mechanics position open with Waco Sales of New York, Roosevelt Field. If you are interested, see Buster Warner of that organization as soon as possible.

Yours very truly,

William C. Erb

William C. Erb, Registrar

WCE:B

A rare letter on Roosevelt Field Inc. stationery dated November 6, 1937 features the highly stylized Roosevelt Field logo.

AIR ASSOCIATES
INCORPORATED
Manufacturers and Distributors of AVIATION MATERIALS AND EQUIPMENT

5300 W. 63RD STREET, CHICAGO, ILL.
1100 AIRWAY DRIVE, GLENDALE, CALIF.

CABLE ADDRESS: AIRSOC, NEW YORK, ALL CODES
OFFICE AND WAREHOUSE BUILDING 19 ROOSEVELT FIELD
GARDEN CITY, N. Y.
PHONES GARDEN CITY 3800 VIGILANT 4-3800

To Our Dealers:

The business of the Nicholas-Beazley Airplane Co., Inc, has been merged with that of Air Associates, Inc. The branch business of the Nicholas-Beazley Airplane Co. at Glendale, California and Floyd Bennett Field, Brooklyn, New York have been transferred to our own Glendale and Garden City offices. The business at Marshall, Missouri and Dallas, Texas will be continued under our name. We now have offices and warehouses at the following five points:

Air Associates, Inc.,
Roosevelt Field,
Garden City, L. I., N. Y.

Air Associates, Inc.,
5300 West 63rd Street
Chicago, Ill.

Air Associates, Inc.,
1100 Airway Drive,
Glendale, Calif.

Air Associates, Inc.,
English at North Street,
Marshall, Mo.

Air Associates, Inc.,
Love Field,
Dallas, Texas

Merchandise shown in the catalog of the Nicholas-Beazley Airplane Co., or previously handled by them, will still be available from any of our five locations. Orders from customers of the Nicholas-Beazley Airplane Co. will receive the same careful attention as before.

Combining the business of the two companies allows larger stocks, a better selection of materials, and improved service to the trade. We again express our appreciation of your past business, and pledge our sincerity in trying to better our service to you through this merger.

Very truly yours,

Air Associates, Inc.

A March 1938 letter to Air Associates dealers explaining their merger with another company. Air Associates was for years an important presence at Roosevelt Field, with a large rectangular building parallel to Clinton Road with the name "Air Associates" written on the roof.

February, 1943 FLYING 293

There is an *unlimited* demand for

ROOSEVELT TRAINED MECHANICS

to help

That is why ROOSEVELT AVIATION SCHOOL is emphasizing its highly specialized

MASTER AIRPLANE AND ENGINE MECHANIC COURSE

as essential Career Training which fits the graduate to meet every requirement for Civilian Employment as a Maintenance Mechanic on Army Airplanes and on Commercial Airplanes.

If it averages *twenty* mechanics to keep *one* airplane in the air, it will take 1,000,000 mechanics to keep 50,000 planes in the air.

No other type of expert is as badly needed as the Master Airplane and Engine Mechanic.

If you want a training that will put you *to* work and keep you *at* work—***now and after the war***—sign and mail the coupon below and ***do it now.***

We can accept only thirty students per month.

1943 Classes Start Monday, January 4, and every fourth Monday thereafter.

SIGN AND MAIL THIS COUPON AND DO IT NOW!

ROOSEVELT AVIATION SCHOOL, At Roosevelt Field, Mineola, L. I., New York

Gentlemen: Without obligating me, please send details regarding your highly specialized

MASTER AIRPLANE AND ENGINE MECHANIC COURSE

Name.. *Age*...............

Street Address..

Town.. *State*...............

P. A. Feb. 1943

An advertisement for the Roosevelt Flying School from February 1943, from the magazine *Flying*, emphasizes the need for airplane mechanics during World War II. For every plane in the air there were trained mechanics needed to keep them flying properly.

A group of twenty-five "Wrens" (Women's Royal Navy Service) from England stationed at Roosevelt Field, photographed on July 31, 1943, having already served five months' time there. Their duties included checking airplanes for Lend-Lease shipment to Britain and related administrative duties. They are seen here in their leisure time at a piano.

Page 6

MUSTER ROLL OF THE CREW

of the U. S. S. Naval Air Facility Roosevelt Field, Mineola, N.Y.

for the quarter ending March 31st, 1943

1 NAMES (Alphabetically arranged without regard to ratings, with surname to the left and the first name written in full)	2 SERVICE NUMBER (The service number must under no condition be omitted)	3 Present Rating	4 DATE OF ENLISTMENT Day	 Month	 Year	5 Date first received on board
PARKHILL, Don Harold	408 88 03	RT3c	Records not on board			1-29-43
SAVARESE, Walter John	708 03 74	RT2c		"		12-17-42
SHAPIRO, Armin Irving	708 09 82	RT2c		"		1-29-43
SINGER, LeRoy (n)	709 73 62	RT3c		"		1-29-43
SOLOMON, Seymour (n)	710 86 70	RT2c		"		1-29-43
TRIGHINGEL, John Freder	708 63 40	RT3c		"		1-29-43
TUSA, Joseph (n)	708 09 08	RT3c		"		1-29-43
VOLK, Edward Warren	710 80 16	RT2c		"		1-29-43
WEINER, Max Jack	709 70 69	RT2c		"		1-29-43
WRONKA, Walter Wenceal	709 87 56	RT3c		"		1-29-43

A muster roll for the quarter ending March 31, 1943, shows some of the men who were stationed at Roosevelt Field's U. S. Naval Air Training Facility.

A British Royal Navy Grumman Tarpon takes off from Roosevelt Field in October 1943 in this British Official Admiralty Photograph. World War II was a team effort and an Allied presence at Roosevelt Field was important just as it had been during World War I.

CIVIL AIR REGULATIONS

PART 01

AIRWORTHINESS CERTIFICATES

As amended to October 15, 1942

CIVIL AERONAUTICS BOARD

WASHINGTON, D. C.

For sale by the Superintendent of Documents, Government Printing Office, Washington 25, D. C. - - - - - Price 5 cents

01.1 AIRWORTHINESS CERTIFICATES

01.10 Application. Application for an airworthiness certificate may be made by the registered owner of any aircraft registered as an aircraft of the United States upon the applicable form prescribed and furnished by the Administrator.

01.11 Requirements for issuance. Prior to the issuance of an airworthiness certificate the subject aircraft shall be inspected by a duly authorized representative for the Administrator to determine whether it is in condition for safe operation and complies with the airworthiness requirements specified in the Civil Air Regulations: *Provided*, That an airworthiness certificate may be issued for an aircraft for which no such certificate has previously been issued and which has been manufactured under type certificate or under a type and a production certificate if the applicant for such certificate, upon request, presents to a duly authorized representative for the Administrator a Statement of Conformity properly executed by the manufacturer of the aircraft on a form prescribed and furnished by the Administrator, and if the aircraft satisfactorily passes an inspection made to determine whether such aircraft is in condition for safe operation: *Provided further*, That an aircraft manufactured under a type certificate only shall undergo, and an aircraft manufactured under a type and a production certificate may be required to undergo, an inspection to determine whether such aircraft conforms to the type certificate under which it is manufactured.

01.12 Aircraft Operation Record requirements. An aircraft for which an airworthiness certificate is currently in effect, hereinafter referred to in these regulations as a certificated aircraft, shall not be operated unless there is attached to such airworthiness certificate the appropriate Aircraft Operation Record prescribed and issued by the Administrator, nor shall such aircraft be operated other than in accordance with the limitations for safe operations prescribed and set forth by the Administrator in such record. An aircraft for which an airworthiness or experimental certificate is in effect on the effective date of this section may be operated without an Aircraft Operation Record until expiration, cancellation, or revocation of any such certificate.

01.13 Duration. An airworthiness certificate shall be of 60 days' duration and, unless the holder thereof is otherwise notified by the Administrator within such period, shall continue in effect indefinitely thereafter, unless suspended, revoked, or cancelled, except that it shall immediately expire (1) at the end of a specifically designated period* after the date of issuance of the certificate or after the date of the last endorsement thereof, whichever is later, if the holder of

*A statement of duration in substantially the form of §01.13 will appear on all airworthiness certificates. The above reference to a "specifically designated period" means the period which will be designated on each airworthiness certificate. Under ordinary circumstances an airworthiness certificate will have to be endorsed each year.

639629—45

A page from the U.S. government's Civil Aeronautics Board's discussion of airplane airworthiness (dated November 1943), part of the materials that students at the Roosevelt Aviation School were given in 1945.

The cover of a binder from the Roosevelt Aviation School, 1945.

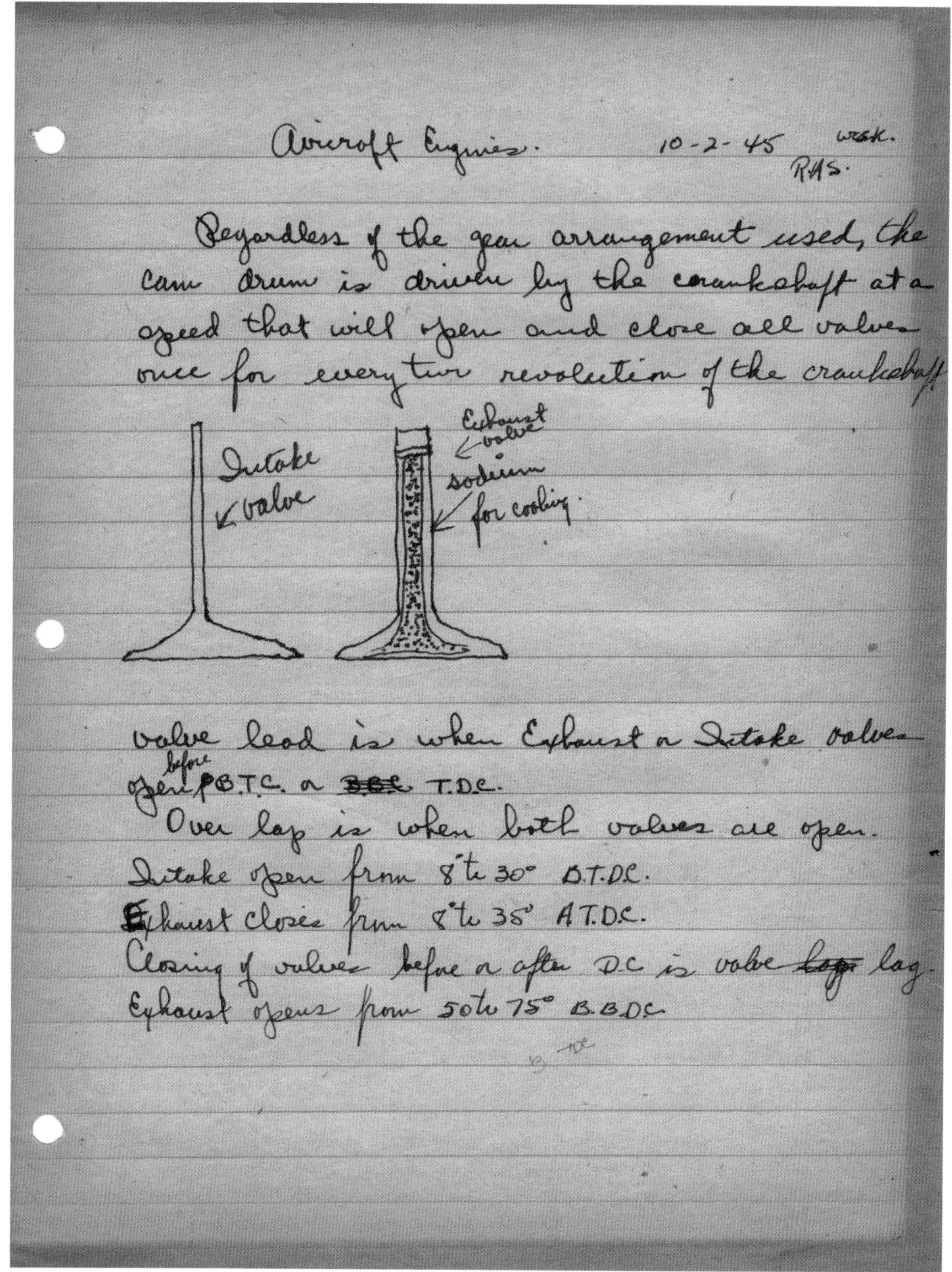

Aircraft Engines. 10-2-45

RHS.

Regardless of the gear arrangement used, the cam drum is driven by the crankshaft at a speed that will open and close all valves once for every two revolution of the crankshaft.

valve lead is when Exhaust or Intake valves open before B.T.C. or ~~B.B.C.~~ T.D.C.

Over lap is when both valves are open.

Intake open from 8° to 30° B.T.D.C.

Exhaust closes from 8° to 35° A.T.D.C.

Closing of valves before or after D.C is valve ~~lap~~ lag.

Exhaust opens from 50 to 75° B.B.D.C.

A page of handwritten notes from a student at the Roosevelt Aviation School, October 1945.

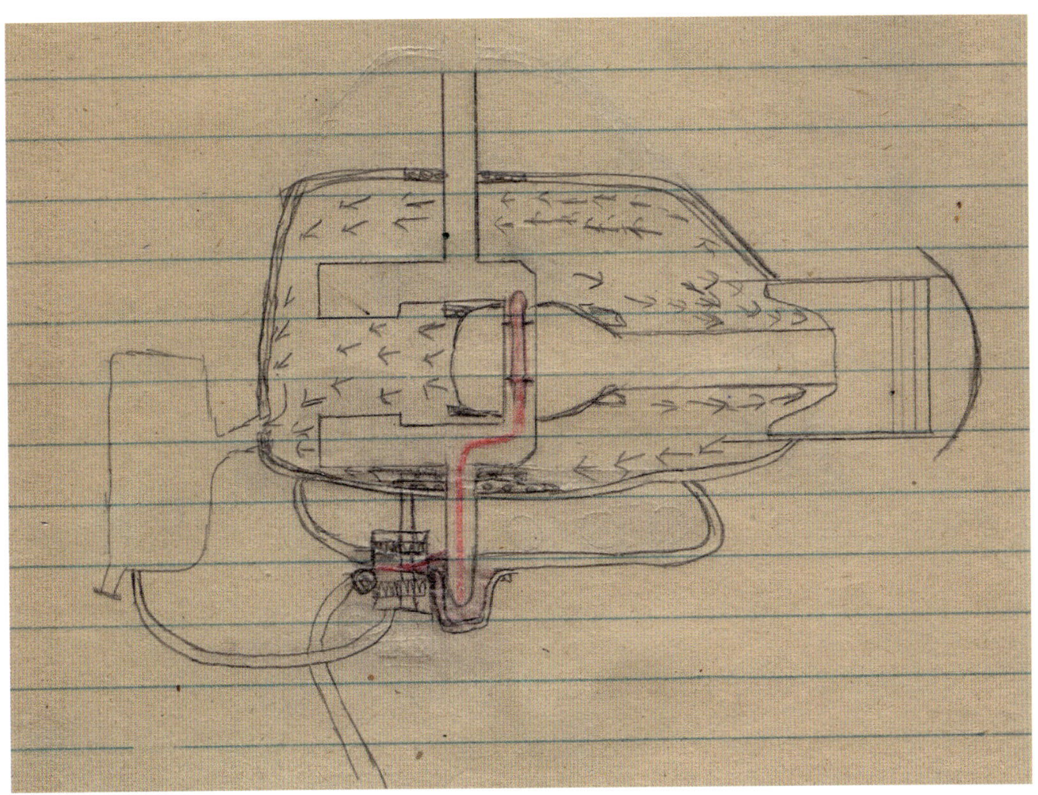

Drawing of an airplane engine by a student at the Roosevelt Aviation School, 1945.

BNP 605-A
(Revised October 1942)

4 OCT 1945

Page 1

MUSTER ROLL OF THE CREW

of the U. S. NAVAL AIR FACILITY, MINEOLA, L.I., NEW YORK

1 OCT 1945

for the quarter ending 30 September, 1945

1 NAMES (Alphabetically arranged without regard to ratings, with surname to the left and the first name written in full)	2 SERVICE NUMBER (The service number must under no condition be omitted)	3 Present Rating	4 DATE OF ENLISTMENT			5 Date first received on board
			Day	Month	Year	

DISESTABLISHED in accordance with SecNav ltr. Op 13 1D psp 29 Aug over Serial 523013 dated 5 September 1945.

Total enlisted personnel received on board from 1 Nov. 1942 to 1 Sept. 1945 - 868

Total enlisted personnel transferred from this station from 27 Nov. 1942 to 22 Sept. 1945 - 868

NO ENLISTED PERSONNEL REMAINING ABOARD.

A government document showing the disestablishment of the U.S Naval Air Facility at Roosevelt Field in October 1945. A total of 868 men were trained at the facility during World War II.

A colorful World War II-era matchbook cover for the Air Forces Training Detachment stationed at Roosevelt Field.

Opposite page: A Consolidated PB4Y-1 heavy bomber & B-24 Consolidated Liberator heavy bomber Load Adjuster Slide Rule dating to the World War II era, made by the Cox & Stevens Aircraft Corporation in Mineola.

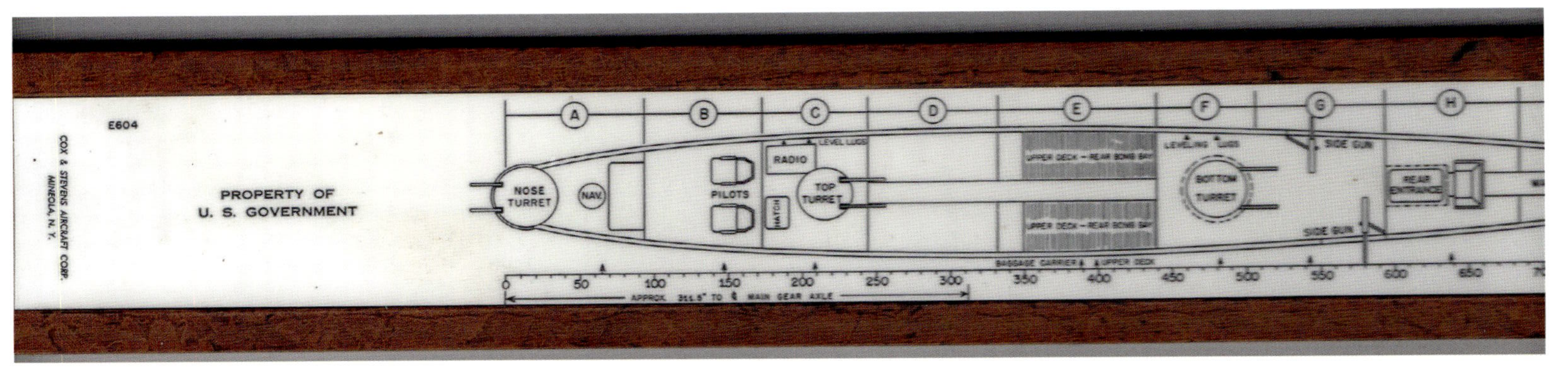

E604
COX & STEVENS AIRCRAFT CORP.
MINEOLA, N. Y.
PROPERTY OF
U. S. GOVERNMENT
NOSE TURRET
NAV.
PILOTS
RADIO
LEVEL LUGS
HATCH
TOP TURRET
UPPER DECK – REAR BOMB BAY
LEVELING LUGS
BOTTOM TURRET
SIDE GUN
REAR ENTRANCE
BAGGAGE CARRIER & UPPER DECK
APPROX. 311.5" TO ℄ MAIN GEAR AXLE

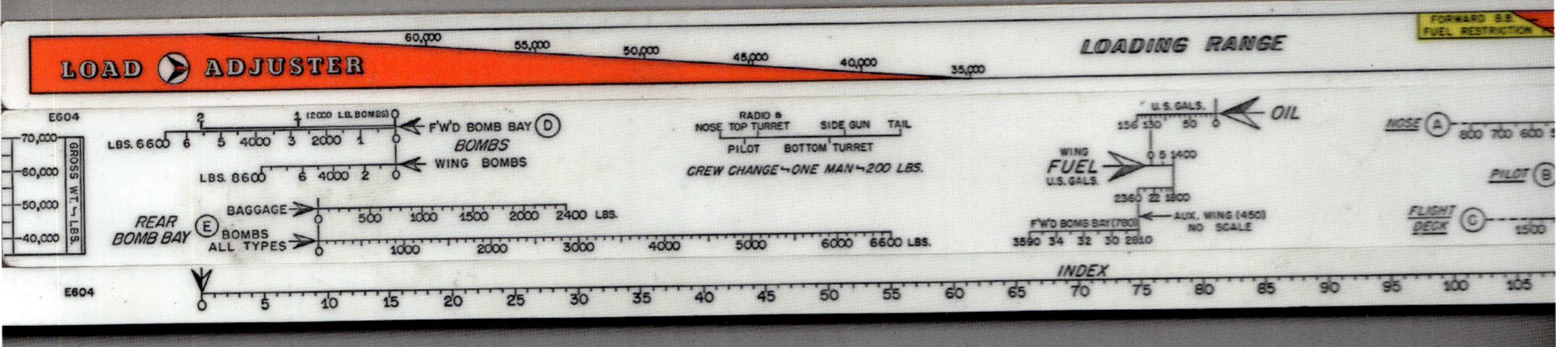

LOAD ADJUSTER
LOADING RANGE
FORWARD B.B. FUEL RESTRICTION
GROSS WT. — LBS.
E604
F'WD BOMB BAY
BOMBS
WING BOMBS
REAR BOMB BAY
BAGGAGE
BOMBS ALL TYPES
NOSE
RADIO & TOP TURRET
SIDE GUN
TAIL
PILOT
BOTTOM TURRET
CREW CHANGE—ONE MAN—200 LBS.
U.S. GALS.
OIL
WING FUEL U.S. GALS.
F'WD BOMB BAY (780)
AUX. WING (450) NO SCALE
PILOT
FLIGHT DECK
INDEX

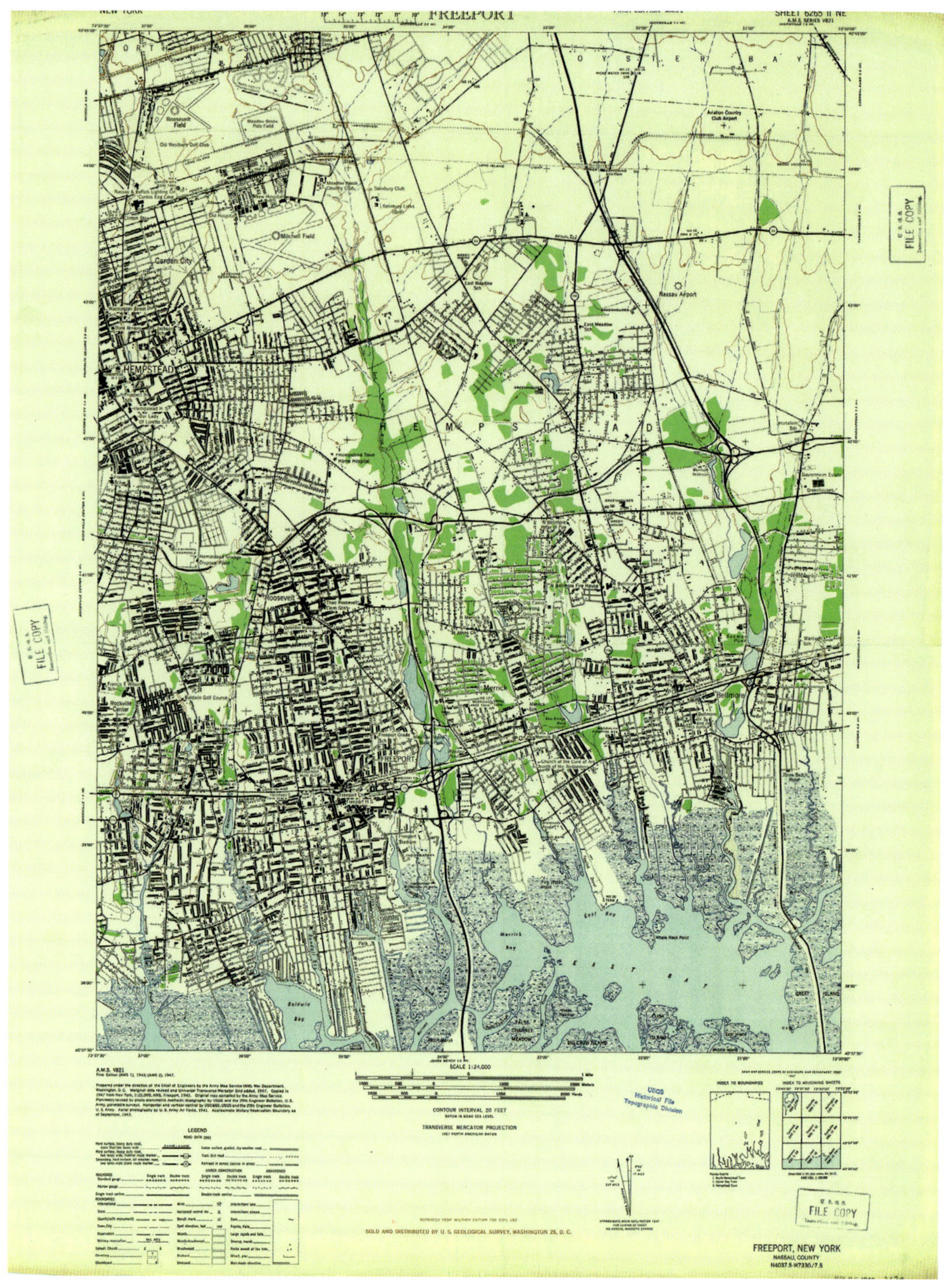

A 1947 USGS topographical map shows Roosevelt Field still extant, though in its last few years of existence. It also gives a good idea of the relative size of Roosevelt Raceway. Note the presence of the Old Westbury Golf Club immediately to the south of the Field.

The front and back of a matchbook for the Roosevelt Field Inn (*circa* late 1940s), which utilized the handsome official Roosevelt Field stylized "R" logo. Though it was used extensively by aviators, the Mineola Kiwanis Club also held frequent events there, such as a Monte Carlo night attended by forty couples in March 1950. The Roosevelt Field Inn burned down in 1953, after the airfield had already closed.

A 1953 image of a race at Roosevelt Raceway shows race results.

This December 1953 aerial view shows a closed Roosevelt Field, with its infrastructure mostly demolished and awaiting new construction of what was to become the Roosevelt Field Mall (and other shopping). The Roosevelt Raceway and the Meadow Brook Polo Field (itself close to closure and demolition) are visible at the right of the image.

A 1955 USGS topographical map of Nassau County shows the drastic changes that happened in the space of just a few years. Roosevelt Airfield is gone, as is the Meadowbrook Polo Field. The Roosevelt Raceway is still there, as is Mitchel Field (misspelled).

The Roosevelt Field shopping center in 1958 was vastly different than the behemoth indoor shopping mall it was to become.

The cover of the program for the 1960 Vanderbilt Cup automobile races held at Roosevelt Raceway and a map of the race course and the program of events (bottom). The 1960 event followed the 1936 and 1937 races held at the same site. The race course occupied what used to be the eastern end of Roosevelt Field.

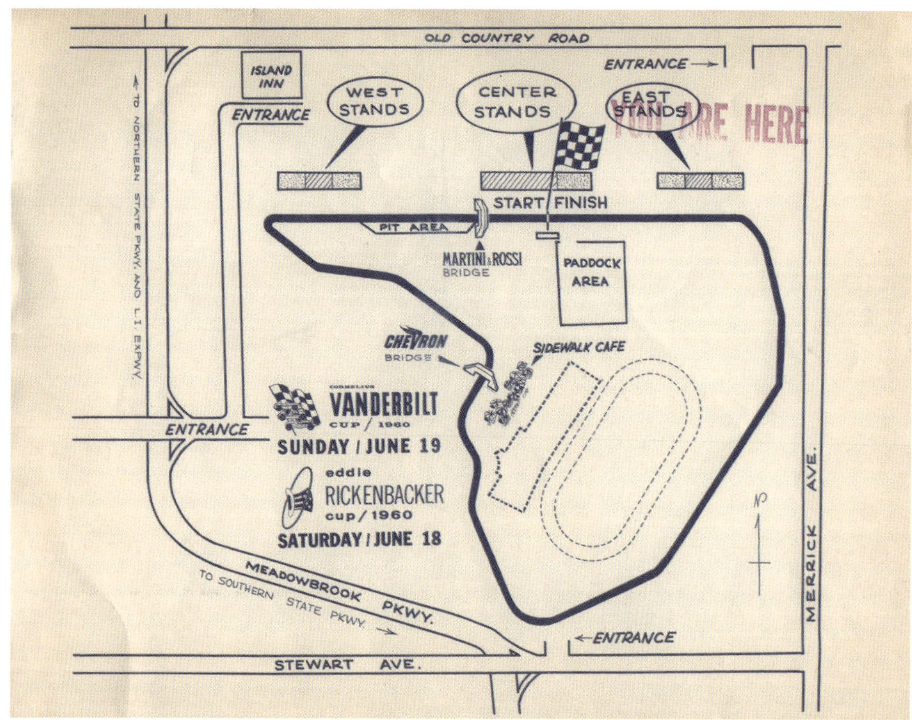

Vice president and Republican presidential nominee Richard Nixon speaking at a campaign stop at Roosevelt Field on November 2, 1960, as President Dwight Eisenhower looks on. It was Nixon vs. John F. Kennedy that year and Nixon went on to lose to Kennedy in the election. In October 1968, Nixon returned to Roosevelt Field as presidential candidate for a brief campaign rally; he won that election.

A first day cover from 1961 celebrating the fiftieth anniversary of Earle Ovington's historic first airmail flight from Garden City to Mineola. Appropriately this envelope was postmarked in Garden City and addressed to Mineola.

SEASON 196.... No 3048

— PASS —

GOOD FOR ONE GAME AT

ROOSEVELT FIELD
MINIATURE GOLF COURSE

Roosevelt Field Shopping Center
Garden City, N. Y.

☐ Free Game
☐ Rain Check
☐ Complimentary

Bill Roesch

AUTHORIZED SIGNATURE
PASS IS NOT VALID UNLESS
PROPERLY SIGNED

The 1969 USGS map of the area shows the continued development of the former airfield site. Note that Mitchel Field is now marked as abandoned. Roosevelt Raceway is still there. Salisbury Park has now been renamed as Eisenhower Memorial Park.

Opposite page:

Above: A *circa* 1960s pass, good for one game of mini golf at Roosevelt Field, a long-gone activity at the mall, which has changed a great deal over the years.

Below: In this 1966 aerial, the Roosevelt Raceway is still visible, but most of what was left of Roosevelt Field is gone (though not completely), replaced by retail. In the years to follow, the area would be completely developed and all the last bits of infrastructure demolished, leaving not a single trace of its previous life.

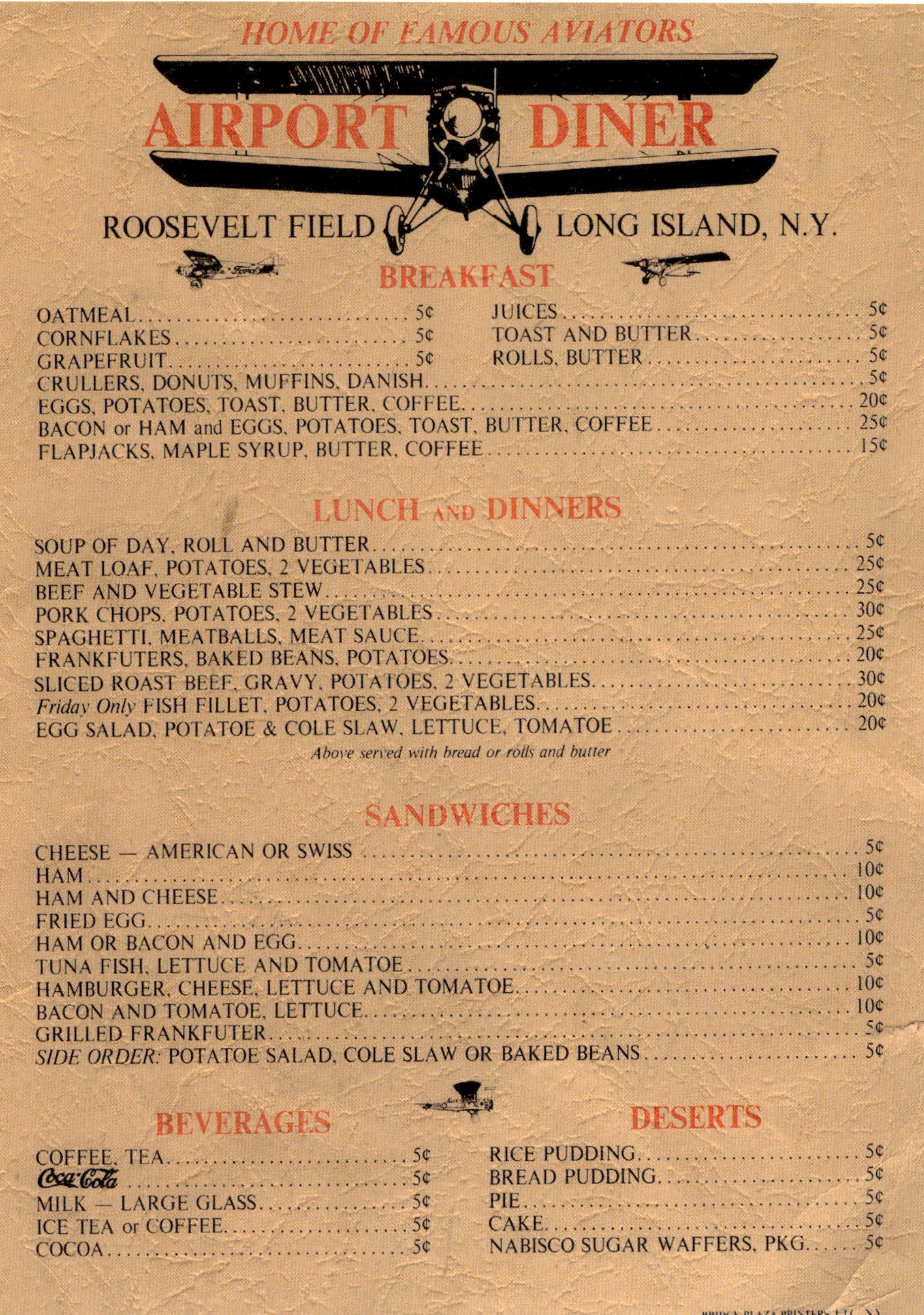

HOME OF FAMOUS AVIATORS

AIRPORT DINER

ROOSEVELT FIELD LONG ISLAND, N.Y.

BREAKFAST

OATMEAL.......... 5¢
CORNFLAKES.......... 5¢
GRAPEFRUIT.......... 5¢
JUICES.......... 5¢
TOAST AND BUTTER.......... 5¢
ROLLS, BUTTER.......... 5¢
CRULLERS, DONUTS, MUFFINS, DANISH.......... 5¢
EGGS, POTATOES, TOAST, BUTTER, COFFEE.......... 20¢
BACON or HAM and EGGS, POTATOES, TOAST, BUTTER, COFFEE.......... 25¢
FLAPJACKS, MAPLE SYRUP, BUTTER, COFFEE.......... 15¢

LUNCH AND DINNERS

SOUP OF DAY, ROLL AND BUTTER.......... 5¢
MEAT LOAF, POTATOES, 2 VEGETABLES.......... 25¢
BEEF AND VEGETABLE STEW.......... 25¢
PORK CHOPS, POTATOES, 2 VEGETABLES.......... 30¢
SPAGHETTI, MEATBALLS, MEAT SAUCE.......... 25¢
FRANKFUTERS, BAKED BEANS, POTATOES.......... 20¢
SLICED ROAST BEEF, GRAVY, POTATOES, 2 VEGETABLES.......... 30¢
Friday Only FISH FILLET, POTATOES, 2 VEGETABLES.......... 20¢
EGG SALAD, POTATOE & COLE SLAW, LETTUCE, TOMATOE.......... 20¢

Above served with bread or rolls and butter

SANDWICHES

CHEESE — AMERICAN OR SWISS.......... 5¢
HAM.......... 10¢
HAM AND CHEESE.......... 10¢
FRIED EGG.......... 5¢
HAM OR BACON AND EGG.......... 10¢
TUNA FISH, LETTUCE AND TOMATOE.......... 5¢
HAMBURGER, CHEESE, LETTUCE AND TOMATOE.......... 10¢
BACON AND TOMATOE, LETTUCE.......... 10¢
GRILLED FRANKFUTER.......... 5¢
SIDE ORDER: POTATOE SALAD, COLE SLAW OR BAKED BEANS.......... 5¢

BEVERAGES

COFFEE, TEA.......... 5¢
Coca-Cola.......... 5¢
MILK — LARGE GLASS.......... 5¢
ICE TEA or COFFEE.......... 5¢
COCOA.......... 5¢

DESERTS

RICE PUDDING.......... 5¢
BREAD PUDDING.......... 5¢
PIE.......... 5¢
CAKE.......... 5¢
NABISCO SUGAR WAFFERS, PKG.......... 5¢

BRIDGE PLAZA PRINTERS L.I.C., N.Y.

An old menu for the "Airport Diner" at Roosevelt Field. Note the several misspellings and also the Coca-Cola logo. There are several of these menus floating around on the internet for sale, yet an extensive search for this diner turns up nothing in the contemporaneous historical records. This is likely a vintage 1960s or later nostalgic creation of a place that never existed.

1927 ★ GOLDEN JUBILEE ★ 1977
FIRST SOLO TRANSATLANTIC FLIGHT

Roosevelt Field, New York
Seconds seemed hours as Charles A. Lindbergh's *Spirit of St. Louis* lumbered aloft for Paris.

ROOSEVELT FIELD STA. N.Y.
MAY 20 1977
11530

A first day cover from 1977 celebrating the fiftieth anniversary of Lindbergh's historic flight, postmarked at Roosevelt Field Station and featuring the newly issued Lindbergh 13-cent stamp. The envelope recreates the scene at Roosevelt Field as Lindbergh took off. The 50th anniversary celebration was held in nearby Eisenhower Park.

The 1994 USGS map of the area. Roosevelt Raceway is still there, but not for much longer.

A somewhat hidden and unassuming stone marker, seen in a 2016 photo, behind the former Source Mall in Westbury, commemorates the spot where Lindbergh's plane became airborne. There is also a sign marking the spot.

A 2021 photo of the Lindbergh plaque, which was moved to its new home in the parking lot of the Cradle of Aviation Museum, south of the original takeoff location.

A 2019 aerial view of what was once Roosevelt Field, looking west toward the spot from where Charles Lindbergh's plane took off in May 1927 on its famous transatlantic flight.

A pair of 2019 views of what was once Roosevelt Field, looking south from Carle Place. This view demonstrates how close residential neighborhoods were to the flying field.

A 2019 aerial view looking north toward the Roosevelt Field Mall from just north of Stewart Avenue.

The original main Curtiss building still stands today, as does the old smokestack behind the building. As of 2019, the building housed a Nassau BOCES operation.

The Roosevelt Field Mall parking lot toward Macy's in June 2020. Roosevelt Field Mall was built on the northwestern end of what was once the flying field.

During the pandemic in 2020, before indoor shopping resumed, the Roosevelt Field parking lot was eerily empty.

The Roosevelt Field Mall actually only occupies a fraction of what was once the Roosevelt Field aviation field. The Trader Joe's seen here in 2020, part of the Gallery at Westbury Plaza, east of the Meadowbrook Parkway, is also on land that was once part of Roosevelt Field.

Looking northeast in 2021, from what was once the westernmost edge of Roosevelt Field, toward 600 Old Country Road.

This grassy area at the northwestern corner of what used to be the airfield, was once the nerve center of Roosevelt Field, a spot where many buildings and hangars, and the pathways between them, stood.

Driving north on Clinton Road and approaching the intersection of Old Country Road before 1951, you'd have passed numerous airfield infrastructure buildings very close to the road on the right side. Now it's just grass and some trees and shrubs.

The remnants of an old wooden fence along the western border of the Roosevelt Field property.

Looking north toward Old Country Road from the largest piece of "untouched" land in the Roosevelt Field property, seen here in 2021. Before 1951, this view would have been crowded with various airfield buildings and hangars lining the west side along Clinton Road and the north side along Old Country Road.

Some glass and ceramic shards found in 2021 at a recently excavated area on the northwestern edge of the Roosevelt Field Mall complex, near Clinton Road. This area was undisturbed for at least fifty-five years and formerly contained Roosevelt Field. Judging from the thickness of the flat glass, it seems to be vintage window glass. Could it be from one of the old hangars or warehouses at Roosevelt Field? Seems possible.

These old concrete construction formwork tie wedges were recently found in an excavated spot at the northwestern corner of the Roosevelt Field property. Iron wedges such as this were used to secure formwork into place to allow poured concrete walls and floors to be straight and level. These almost definitely date to the construction of the old concrete hangars at the field. Were they stored on site for use on various construction projects around Roosevelt Field? Quite possibly, since this was not the type of thing that would normally be abandoned. They'd come off with the formwork after the concrete was dry, and Roosevelt Field leased space to its tenants so would have perhaps had its own construction crew on hand for various projects. In fact, the location where these were found corresponds to the old Roosevelt Field storage building. Wedges like this have since been replaced with much smaller and lighter versions as concrete construction has evolved over the years.